Advanced Listening
Comprehension

Advanced Listening Comprehension

DEVELOPING LISTENING AND NOTE-TAKING SKILLS

Patricia Dunkel/Frank Pialorsi

Center for English as a Second Language
University of Arizona

NEWBURY HOUSE PUBLISHERS
A division of HarperCollins*Publishers*

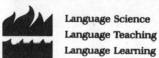

Language Science
Language Teaching
Language Learning

91-859

Library of Congress Cataloging in Publication Data

Dunkel, Patricia.
    Advanced listening comprehension.

    Summary: Introduces the fundamentals of listen-
ing and note-taking using written exercises and
audio activities.
        1.   English language--Text-books for foreigners.
2.   Listening.   3.   Note-taking.   [1.   English
language--Textbooks for foreigners.   2.   Listening.
3.   Note-taking]   I.   Pialorsi, Frank.   II.   Title.
PE1128.D827   428.3'4   81-18998
ISBN 0-88377-227-2   AACR2

Illustrations by Jackson Boelts

Cover and interior book design by Edith Allard of Designworks

NEWBURY HOUSE PUBLISHERS
A division of Harper & Row, Publishers, Inc.

NEWBURY HOUSE PUBLISHERS
A division of HarperCollins*Publishers*

CAMBRIDGE, MASSACHUSETTS

First printing: March 1982
Printed in the U.S.A.
14 15 16 17

Acknowledgments

Our gratitude is expressed to the many students of the University of Arizona's Center for English as a Second Language, and to the summer-session students at Georgetown University who participated in the field-testing of the material. Their comments and suggestions helped shape portions of the book. We extend deep appreciation to our colleagues at the Center who were often mentors as well as monitors of the creative process: Gary Vanca, Gary Johnston, and Melinda Curry; to William Norris of Georgetown University. We are particularly grateful for the support and encouragement that Ernestine Neff, the former Director of the Center, gave to the entire project. We especially want to thank Loretta and John Graney, Tania and Bruce Dunkel and Leyla and Pia Pialorsi, to whom this work is dedicated. Thanks also are expressed to Robert Rosaldo, our audio-assistance technician, for all his assistance, patience and humor during the taping of the lectures.

Preface

Much of the research concerning the efficacy of lecture note-taking indicates that information acquired during an oral presentation that is configured in some meaningful written form is remembered far longer than information that is not written down at all. Studies such as those of Howe (1970) and Weiland and Kingsbury (1979), for example, have shown that subjects who took notes during a taped presentation performed significantly better on a subsequent multiple-choice test than did subjects in a no note-taking control group.

It is too often presumed that anyone who considers doing degree work at a college or university where English is the language of instruction possesses the requisite ability to listen to a lecture in English and to take notes on it. Since the lecture method is so pervasive in institutions of higher education and is such an integral part of the American instructional process, and since the student is generally tested on material presented, or even just mentioned, by the professors during class lectures and discussions, good listening and note-taking skills become really a question of survival for the college student.

Professors usually assume that their students "know" how to take notes. And yet, surprisingly, the vast majority, including both native-speakers and foreign students, begin their college work with absolutely no formal instruction in developing the art of taking good notes on oral presentations. Perhaps one reason for this oversight is the illusion held by teachers and students alike that the skill of lecture note-taking is absorbed automatically—osmotically, one might say—as the students progress through U.S. high schools or intensive English programs to go on to the undergraduate and graduate programs in American colleges and universities. But is the skill really absorbed by osmosis? Both university educators and their students should seriously question the validity of this notion of osmosis.

The authors are convinced that college-bound students, and especially college-bound foreign students, need training and practice in developing extended listening comprehension and note-taking skills. We designed and wrote *Advanced Listening Comprehension* with this as the primary objective—to give the training and practice needed in listening and note-taking in English. The material has been scripted to provide a speaker-mentor to guide the student along in listening and note-taking skill development. The mentor interrupts the lecturers in the early presentations to inquire whether or not the important facts were noted down. Opportunity for self-correction is given, and encouragement frequently offered, so that the learner can begin to develop simultaneously both confidence and skill in listening and note-taking in English. The project also aims to build a bridge between the language of the "linguistically sheltered" ESL classroom, where the emphasis is on language training, and the demanding discourse of the university lecture hall, emphasizing content and skill mastery.

ORGANIZATION OF THE BOOK

Introduction

Advanced Listening Comprehension is a program for high-intermediate and advanced students of English as a second language who seek to improve their listening comprehension of English and their note-taking skills. Fifteen lectures guide the students along in this endeavor.

Aside from developing note-taking ability, several other interlocking skills necessary for academic success are worked on in tandem: (1) processing information received aurally; (2) making inferences and drawing conclusions therefrom; (3) becoming familiar with the various styles and accents of lecturers; (4) handling objective test-taking formats (a testing section after each lecture familiarizes the students with the objective-test format often used in tests of listening comprehension); and (5) preparing for classroom discussion and debates. (The questions in the discussion and writing module can be worked on with the aid of an instructor.) Each question or statement revolves around a topic or theme related to the lecture.

SCHEMA OF THE BOOK

A. Pre-listening Activities

I. *Introduction to the Lecture*
   — Preview of Content (Lectures 1–15)
   — Lecture Outline (Lectures 9–15)
   — Preview of Vocabulary (Lectures 1–13)
   — Preview of Sentences (Lectures 1–15)

Preview of Content presents a short, general description of the theme and organization of the lecture.

Lecture Outline blueprints the organization of the longer lectures by breaking down the selection into its parts and by showing the interrelationship among the parts. Two types of outlines are used: sentence outlines, in which the ideas of the lecture appear in sentence form; and topic outlines, in which the ideas appear in word, phrase, or clause form.

Preview of Vocabulary highlights selected low-frequency and lecture-specific vocabulary items. General definitions are presented, and the student is instructed to match each definition with the correct item by filling in the blanks with the matching word or phrase given. The process of elimination should assist the student in figuring out the meaning of most unfamiliar items.

Preview of Sentences places the Preview of Vocabulary items in the context in which they occur in the lecture presentation.

B. Listening Activities

II. *Lecture Presentation*
— Note-taking Model (Lectures 1–10) *ON TAPE*
— Lecture Overview (Lectures 11–13) *ON TAPE*
— Note-taking Exercise (Lectures 1–15) *ON TAPE*

Note-taking Model (Lectures 1–10) outlines the lecture in skeleton form. The student listens to the lecture while looking at the model. The model contains only the necessary content words contained in the lecture, along with any essential structure words. It contains abbreviations and symbols to highlight the importance of reducing aurally received information to a briefer, written form. The student is advised to follow the form and outline of the model insofar as information reduction and use of abbreviations and symbols are concerned. The listener is, however, also advised to develop an individual style of note-taking that will best suit his or her individual needs. The entire lecture is given at a normal rate of delivery and without interruption (i.e., without the prompting assistance given during the early Note-taking Exercise presentations).

Lecture Overview (Lectures 11–13) replaces the Note-taking Model used in Lectures 1–10. The student, by this time, has become familiar with the concept and structure of a note-taking model. The lectures have increased in length and complexity so the student is now given a short overview which elaborates upon and expands both the Preview of Content and Lecture Outline. A synopsis of the content of the lecture and the organizational strategy adopted by the speaker is given.

Note-taking Exercise (Lectures 1–15) requires that the student take notes on the information contained in the lecture as the lecture is given. During presentation of the early lectures (Lectures 1–8), a speaker-mentor guides the listener's note-taking by interrupting the lecture presentation at suitable breaks in the lecture to help the student jot down the most important information. The student is given the opportunity to add any information missed during the initial presentation. This prompting aims (1) to highlight the noteworthy information contained in the lecture, which is usually dense with content words, and to show the student how to avoid taking down nonessential or redundant content presented; and (2) to build up the student's confidence in his or her ability to listen and take notes in English simultaneously. The student is gradually weaned from this prompting, and given the opportunity (once confidence and skill are developed) to take notes without prompting or interruption on the longer and more detailed lecture presentations.

C. Post-listening Activities

III. *Testing Section*
     — Multiple-Choice Questions (Lectures 2–15)   *ON TAPE*
     — True–False Statements (Lectures 2–15)

ON TAPE

Multiple-Choice Questions test (1) whether or not the facts (dates, measurements, statistics, etc.) were accurately recorded in note form; in other words, they test whether or not the lecture information was *stored* properly; (2) they test whether or not the student can *retrieve* the information which was stored earlier in note form; that is, whether or not the information stored can be *found* and *interpreted*; and (3) they test whether or not simple calculations, using the data which was stored and retrieved, can be computed correctly.

True–False Statements test the student's (1) understanding of information presented in paraphrased form; (2) ability to make inferences and draw logical conclusions based on the data given; (3) ability to distinguish between logical deductions drawn from the information presented, and purely speculative guesses not founded upon fact.

D. Follow-up Activities

IV. *Discussion and Writing Section*
     — Topics for Discussion and Writing (Lectures 1–15)

Topics for Discussion and Writing parallel themes covered in the lecture, but require the student to reorganize, synthesize, or amplify the data given. The questions often call for a subjective reaction on the part of the student, or they may call for a detached analysis. Some require that outside reference sources be consulted in preparing answers to the questions. Many of the questions attempt to familiarize the student with the vocabulary of expository writing and speaking by using terms like *evaluate, state, trace the development of, illustrate, analyze, compare,* and *contrast.* The teacher should be sure that the student understands the meaning and use of these terms in exposition.

V. *Lecture Scripts and Answer Keys*
These are printed at the back of the book.
— Lecture Scripts (Lectures 1–15)
— Answer Keys (Lectures 1–15)

Lecture Scripts can be previewed before the student listens to the lectures or can be used as visual reinforcement to back up the oral-aural work which went before. (If the tapes are not available for classroom or individual use, the instructor can use the scripts to present the lectures to the students.)

Answer Keys contain the answers to (1) the Preview of Vocabulary, (2) the Multiple-Choice Questions, and (3) the True–False Statements. The instructor may wish to withhold access to the Keys from the students, or may wish to encourage students to work through the lessons on their own and at their own pace. The material can thus be used in a teacher-directed instructional setting, or in a self-instructional setting (with the tapes).

SUGGESTIONS FOR TEACHING WITH THE MATERIAL

Teachers and classes vary enormously, so naturally each teacher must bring to the instructional situation all of his or her own insight, training, and experience to supplement the material contained in the book. Although the course was designed with a progressive sequencing in mind, the material still lends itself to flexibility of approach. The teacher may reorder segments of the lessons as it seems desirable to do so.

Supplementing the book with additional media programs would be beneficial to the students. Viewing film strips, slide-tape presentations, 16 mm films, and videotapes on lecture topics would expand their lexicon still further, and would expose them to different speech styles and accents. After working through the lecture on the Panama Canal (Lecture 8), for instance, the teacher might arrange for the students to view a film or film strip dealing with the history and construction of the Panama or the Suez Canal.

An Introduction to Listening and Note-taking: Why and What (p. xix)

Begin by asking some general questions about taking notes while listening: "When you watch television do you take notes? Why not?" "Does a secretary take notes when the boss is dictating a letter? Why?" "Do newsmen and newswomen take notes when an important political figure gives a speech? Why do they?" "What are the differences in the note-taking approaches used in these situations?" Discuss the lecture format of classes in which a professor lectures and students listen and take notes. Turn on the tape of the lecture, or read the script. Have the students follow along in their books during the reading. After the students have listened once, have them listen to the entire lecture again with their books closed. Check their comprehension of the content and language by questioning them: Ask them to list the reasons why listening and taking notes is beneficial; dictate the list of words or phrases given in the script and ask the students to write down the symbols used for these words or phrases (see page xxi). Then give them an additional short piece of information and ask them to take notes on it. You might use a short paragraph from a newspaper article. You might dictate a paragraph in English and ask the students to take notes on it in their native language. Ask them to read back the paragraph in English. Do they have difficulty doing so? Then read another short paragraph for them in English, and ask them to take notes on it *in English.* Can they reconstruct the notes they took in English more rapidly or less rapidly than the notes they took in their native language? Keep the paragraphs of equal difficulty in terms of content and language.

FOLLOWING THE FORMAT OF UNITS 1-15

A. Pre-listening Activities

Preview of Content (Lectures 1–15). Read the Preview aloud and have the students follow along in their books. Or ask the students to read the Preview sometime before they come to class, for homework.

Lecture Outline (Lectures 9–15). Ask the students to read and study the Outline for a few minutes. Ask them to close their books and to reconstruct the Outline from memory. Have them compare their reconstructed Outline with the one in the book. Then discuss the relationship between the main topics and the subtopics.

Preview of Vocabulary (Lectures 1–13). Explain the task to the students, and then allow them time to work through the exercise by themselves.

Encourage students to use the process of elimination to help narrow the field in guessing the meanings of items they are not familiar with. Check their answers when they have finished.

Preview of Sentences (Lectures 1–15). Ask students to read through the sentences, or read the sentences aloud and ask them to follow along in their books. In Lectures 14 and 15 the Preview of Sentences is on tape. Have the students listen to the sentences while reading them. Then ask them to try to repeat the sentences from memory. Assure the students that they may not be able to repeat the sentences word for word, but they should attempt to reconstruct them as best they can.

B. Listening Activities

Note-taking Model (Lectures 1–10). Turn on the tape or read the script at the end of the book. Ask the students to follow the model (but not the script) in their books.
   a. Ask the students to uncover the model line by line with paper or a ruler as they listen to the information presented.
   b. Write, or have one of the students write, sections of the model on the chalkboard, and ask the students to reconstruct complete statements from these notations.
   c. Ask the students to list the symbols used in the model and to explain what the symbols stand for.
   d. Check whether or not the students used symbols different from the ones found in the model. Discuss the differences.
   e. Dictate several words from the lecture, and ask the students to abbreviate these words. Check their abbreviations.

Lecture Overview (Lectures 11–13). One of several approaches may be taken:
   a. Have the students turn to the Lecture Overview script and read along as the Overview is presented (for lower-level students).
   b. Have the students close their books and listen while the Overview is given.
   c. Have the students listen to the Overview while looking at the Lecture Outline.
   d. Have the students take notes on the main points listed in the Overview.

Note-taking Exercise (Lectures 1–15). The lecture is given (either on tape or as read by the teacher). If the students have difficulty keeping up with the pace of the tape, stop the tape and allow them to check their progress. Adequate prompting is given the students in the early lectures. Extend the prompting beyond Lecture 8 if necessary.

Ask the students to purchase notebooks (or at least to set aside one section of a notebook) for taking notes using *Advanced Listening Comprehension.* Instruct them to record the title of the lecture, the date notes were taken, and so on. This should encourage the neatness and organization necessary to keep a useful lecture notebook.

C. Post-listening Activities

Testing Section (Lectures 2–15). One of two approaches may be taken:
  a. Have the students take the test just as soon as they have worked through the Note-taking Exercise. Immediate recall of lecture content will be high. (It may be advantageous to use this approach with the first several lectures.)
  b. Have the students take the test a day or several days after the Note-taking Exercise has been completed. This will emphasize the storage function of the note-taking process, and will lessen the impact of immediate recall of the content on the test scores. (Following this approach becomes more necessary as the lectures increase in length and complexity, since the time spent working through the lectures increases.)

Multiple-choice Questions. Each question is read twice, but is not written out for the students. Only the choices appear in the exercise section. Suggest that students preview the answer choices before they listen to each question. Ask them to listen carefully to the question, and then to check their notes taken during the Note-taking Exercise to locate the information that will yield the correct answer; then to select the best answer to the question posed.

True–False Statements. Request the students to work through this exercise on their own, and then check their answers.

Check the answers orally with the students, or collect the papers and grade them as quizzes. Check whether or not the students had difficulty (1) understanding the questions; (2) locating the answers to the questions in the notes they took; (3) making inferences about the content of the lectures; or (4) making elementary calculations using the data.

D. Follow-up Activities

Discussion and Writing Section (Lectures 1–15). The topics can be handled in several ways. The instructor should:
  a. Have the students prepare oral answers to one or more of the questions for homework, and then to be prepared to present their answers to the class the next day.
  b. Have the students prepare written answers to the questions and discussion topics in paragraph or composition form.
  c. Have the students tape-record their responses to the questions, and review the tapes with them the following day in class.
  d. Have the students take opposing sides and prepare arguments for the several lecture topics that lend themselves to debate.

References

Berliner, D. C. The effects of test-like events and notetaking on learning from lecture instruction. Unpublished doctoral dissertation, Stanford University, 1968.

Howe, M. J. A. Using students' notes to examine the role of the individual learner in acquiring meaningful subject matter. *Journal of Educational Research,* 1970, *64,* 61–63.

Weiland, A., and Kingsbury, S. J. Immediate and delayed recall of lecture material as a function of notetaking. *Journal of Educational Resarch,* 1979, *72* (4), 228–230.

Schema

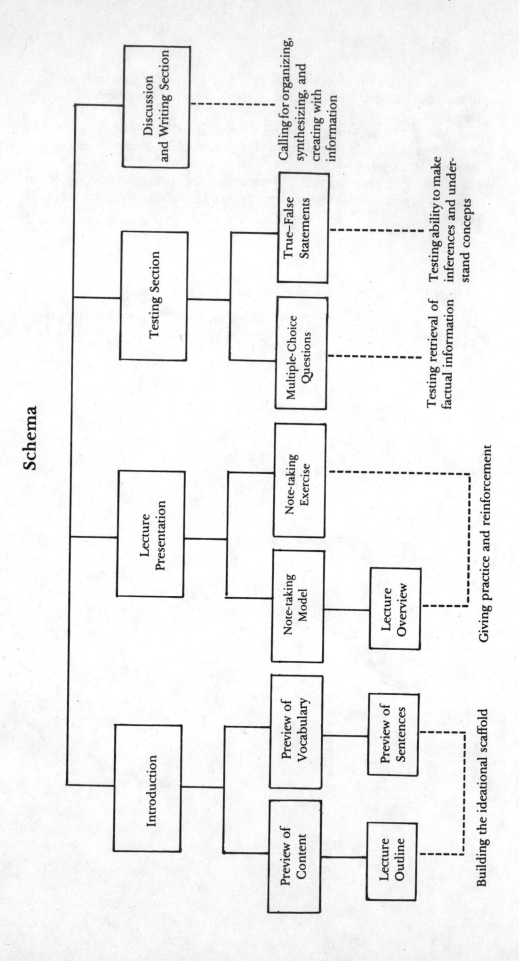

Contents

AN INTRODUCTION TO LISTENING
AND NOTE-TAKING: WHY AND WHAT

Note-taking is a common practice at colleges and universities where English is the language of instruction. Taking notes on lectures is an accepted part of the American college scene. It is quite usual to see college students entering class carrying notebooks in which to take notes on material presented there. Taking notes while listening to a lecture benefits students in several ways. First, the notes provide a record of the information discussed by the professor in class, information that the professor believes is especially important for students to learn. Very often the professor points out or highlights certain information contained in an assignment which the students had to read outside class. It is important to have this highlighted information available to study before an examination. So, in many ways, your class notebook stores the information as a computer does. It holds the information for you until you need it for study or review. This is often called the "recording and storing information" function of note-taking. It is one of the important reasons for learning to take good notes on lectures.

Another advantage of taking notes while listening in class is that it forces you to pay closer attention to the class lecture or discussion. If you listen passively to a professor who is talking on and on for an hour or so, your mind will often wander and your attention lessen. You are sitting in class and listening, but that may be all you are doing; however, when you listen *actively*—that is, when you are listening and taking notes on what you are listening to—you have to pay more careful and constant attention to what is being said. This is because you are trying to transform what you hear into an understandable, abbreviated written form. As a foreign student, you may find it very difficult to listen and write notes in English at the same time. It *is* difficult at first, but you will learn how to do so with practice. You may be afraid you will forget what you are listening to because you are listening and writing at the same time, but the studies of researchers such as Andrea Weiland and Steven Kingsbury, and David Berliner, on the value of note-taking in learning lecture material have shown that learners remember information they have reproduced in some note form much better than lecture information they have listened to but did not take down in note form. So doing two things at the same time—listening and taking notes—is better than doing one thing at a time. We do not say it is easier; we say it is better.

Of course, there is no one method of taking notes that is best for everybody. Note-taking is an individual thing, and you must develop a method that works for you. With practice, you will develop your own system. Now, how do you begin to learn to take good lecture notes in

START THE TAPE.

English? First, of course, you must know English well enough to understand what the professor is saying. Then you must pick out the most important points of the information presented. After that, you must quickly write down these main points in your notebook. You may ask how you do all this at once, and in a foreign language. Practice will help you develop this ability. Remember, just as it takes time and exposure to learn a foreign language, it also takes time and practice to learn how to take notes in that foreign language.

Now, let's talk about what note-taking is really all about. It is extremely important in note-taking to know what you need to write down and what you don't need to write down. You should write down only the most important words; the words that carry the most information; words like nouns, verbs, numbers, statistics, dates, and names of places and people. We call these words *content words*. In general, you don't need to write down articles, such as *the, an,* and so forth, and most prepositions, unless they signal an important time change. For example, you would have to note the prepositions in the expression, "before 1950" and "after World War II." Prepositions and articles are called *structure words*.

In lecture note-taking, you must also learn to ignore, or not to write down, information that is repeated by the lecturer. A professor will often repeat the same information with different words. It is good to hear the information presented in two ways, but it is not a good idea to write down the repeated information. Remember, write down only the information-carrying or content words, and ignore repeated items.

As for selecting the most important words, how do you determine what the most important words are? Listen to the following piece of information:

"The President of the United States arrived back in Washington, D.C. late in the evening of Monday, July 6th. His trip took him to the Middle Eastern country of Saudi Arabia where he took part in several meetings about the price of oil and world-wide inflation."

It is quite obvious that you cannot write down every word that you just heard. Not only would it be impossible to do so, but also it would not be necessary. The entire message can be reduced to the following key words:

President United States arrived D.C. Monday July 6.
Trip Saudi Arabia meetings about price oil world inflation.

Notice that the pronouns, articles, most prepositions, and obvious words have been omitted in the written form. This is very important to do when you are taking notes because you don't have the time to write down every word that you hear.

Now, let's consider that same message again:

President United States arrived D.C. Monday July 6.
Trip Saudi Arabia meetings about price oil world inflation.

It would take quite a while to get even key or content words down on paper just as they are. What can be done to shorten the time it takes to write down these key words? You can use abbreviations and symbols.

Take a minute to note the abbreviations and symbols we have used for the same message:

Pres. U.S. arriv. D.C. Mon. 7/6

Trip — S.A. meetings re pr. oil + world infl.

Notice the symbol "re." It is a common symbol for the prepositions *about* and *concerning.* There are several common symbols that can be used effectively in taking notes. Other such symbols are the "plus" sign (+) or the "and" sign (&).

You may want to develop your own set of symbols to use when taking notes. The only requirements are that the symbols make sense to you and that you use them consistently.

Here are some symbols that are often used in lecture note-taking. Look at the list.

=	equals; is the same as
≠	does not equal; is different from; is not the same as
>	is greater than; is more than
<	is less than
→	causes; results in
←	is caused by; resulted in
re	about; concerning
e.g.	for example
i.e.	that is; for example (also)
∴	therefore
$	money
%	percent

You may want to use certain symbols that are meaningful only for you. Go right ahead and do so. Just be careful that you don't create so many symbols and abbreviations in your notes that they become confusing and hard to understand.

Now, practice listening to a short passage while you try to take down the most important words. Remember, use abbreviations and symbols when you can.

_____

_____

_____

_____

Check to be sure that you wrote down these words:

N.Y. Times — 1900 — 20% Am. wk. force — women
        today — 40% " " " "

A very important symbol in good note-taking is the ditto mark ("). You will save yourself a lot of time by using it to indicate that the word above it is being repeated or used again.

Did you also notice that the lecturer repeated the fact that back in the year 1900, only 20% of the American work force was made up of women when she said the following: "In other words, 20% of all the workers in the United States were women." As we said before, this repeating or expanding of information is very common in lecture language and does not need to be written down again.

Which words that you heard did you not include in your written notes? Why weren't they included? Think about these two points for a minute.

(Remember, this is one way of arranging and reducing the information to written form. You may have done something slightly different. Did you, however, get down all the facts, and could you reconstruct the notes into sentences if you had to?)

STOP THE TAPE.   THIS IS THE END OF THE INTRODUCTORY LECTURE.

NOTE-TAKING EXERCISE

SCRIPT

According to a recent article in the New York Times newspaper, back in the year 1900, only 20 percent of the American work force was made up of women. In other words, 20 percent of all workers in the United States were women. Today, however, at least 40 percent of the nation's work force is made up of women.

Advanced Listening Comprehension

The United Nations:
The Promise of Peace

An Introduction to the Lecture
and to Note-Taking

A. Pre-listening Activities

PREVIEW OF CONTENT

Many people already know what the United Nations Organization is and where it is located, but how many know when and why it was first planned?

In this lecture, the answers to these questions are explored, and some recent statistics about its operating budget are given.

PREVIEW OF VOCABULARY

Before you listen to the lecture on the United Nations, it will be helpful to preview some of the vocabulary and sentences that are used in the lecture. You will first be given several vocabulary items in isolation. Below each group of items are sentence definitions for each. You are to fill in the blanks with the appropriate vocabulary items from the list. Use your dictionary if necessary to select the correct item for each sentence definition. After you have worked through the Preview of Vocabulary, you will be given the Preview of Sentences. The highlighted vocabulary words are presented in the same context in which they are used in the lecture.

---

pledge   headquarters   charter

---

1. The main office of an organization is its _____ .

2. To promise sincerely is to _____ .

3. The constitution of the United Nations Organization is known as its _____ .

---

lend   philanthropist   nuclear weapons   budget

---

4. To give money on the condition that it be repaid at a later date is to _____ money.

5. A _____ is a very rich person who gives money for good causes, such as education and medical research.

6. A _____ is a list of income and expenses for a certain period of time.

7. Instruments of war that use atomic energy are known as _____ .

CHECK YOUR ANSWERS.

PREVIEW OF SENTENCES

Here are some of the sentences you will encounter in the lecture.

1. The United Nations *headquarters* is in the United States, in New York City.

2. In 1944 twenty-six countries *pledged* to continue to fight against Germany and Italy in World War II.

3. The *charter* of the U.N. was formally signed by fifty countries in October of 1945 in San Francisco, California.

4. In 1950 John D. Rockefeller, Jr., the well-known oil millionaire and *philanthropist,* gave the United Nations Organization a section of land in New York City.

5. The United States government *lent* the U.N. $65 million to construct a building to house the international organization.

6. The United Nations budget now totals more than $450 million per year.

7. It is so vital, so really necessary, that countries settle disputes or disagreements in this day of world-wide *nuclear weapons.*

B. Listening Activities

NOTE-TAKING MODEL

START THE TAPE.

Now you are going to listen to a lecture about the United Nations. While you listen, look at the Note-Taking Model on page 5. It is a model of the way you might want to organize your notes on the lecture if you were taking notes on it. Remember, this is just one way in which the notes can be organized and written down. You must develop your own method of taking notes on lectures in English. You must be sure, however, that you write down all the important words, numbers, dates, names, and so forth.

Notice that the model contains only the most important words, numbers, dates, and names in the lecture. The model also contains many abbreviations and several symbols.

After you have listened to the lecture once while looking at this model, you will have a chance to take notes on the information. Now, just listen and look at the model.

The United Nations: The Promise of Peace

U.N.   — 141 cos.
              purp.   — orig. purpose   — peace + coop.
              hdqtr. — NYC
              branch — Paris, Rome, Geneva
              '44   —1st planned
              "   — 26 cos. →fight Germ. + Italy   — WW II

chart.   — 10/45 — 50 "   — S.F. Calif.
              '50   — Rockefeller   — oil phil. →land (NYC)
                      — U.S. govt.   — $65 m.   — building

today   — 73 hect. (18 acres)   —   NYC

budget   — +$450 m./yr.
              U.S. 25%
              USSR 12.9%
              Japan 7.15%
              Fr. 5.86%

no-str. U.N.

co. joins U.N. — prom.   — settle disp. peacefully
                "   — n. easy   — keep
                "   — nec.   — nuc. weap.

All right, let's talk about the symbols used in the Note-Taking Model for a minute. Did you understand what the symbols meant? The + symbol, of course, meant *and*—"international peace *and* international cooperation." The use of an apostrophe (') before two numbers indicates a date, a twentieth-century date. '44 is, therefore, 1944. The ditto sign (") was used to indicate that the number above it was being repeated. Several other symbols were used. Circle three other symbols that were used in the model. What do the symbols mean? Did you also note the use of the dash (–) in the model? It can help you show a relationship between words or groups of words. It indicates that certain words have been omitted, words such as prepositions, and so forth.

NOTE-TAKING EXERCISE

You are now going to hear the lecture again, and you will practice taking notes on what you hear. Remember, write down only the important words. Use symbols and abbreviate as many words as you can. Before you begin, look at the *Word Guide*. These are examples of words that the lecturer might write on the blackboard before or during the lecture.

Word Guide

the United Nations / New York City / Paris / Rome / Geneva / Germany / Italy / San Francisco, California / John D. Rockefeller, Jr. / the Soviet Union / Japan / France

_____

_____

_____

_____

_____

_____

_____

_____

_____

_____

_____

_____

_____

_____

_____

_____

_____

_____

_____

_____

_____

This is the end of the taped section of Lecture 1.

STOP THE TAPE.

C. Post-listening Activities

TOPICS FOR DISCUSSION OR WRITING

1. Do you think that the United Nations headquarters should be located in New York City? If you think it should, why do you feel this way? If you think that it should not be, why do you feel this way? Where do you think it should be located?

2. In an encyclopedia or an almanac, look up the following information about the United Nations and write out the answers.

   What is the function of:
   a. the United Nations General Assembly
   b. the United Nations Secretariat
   c. UNESCO
   d. UNICEF

3. In your opinion, is there any country that the United Nations should refuse to admit as a member? Explain.

The Weather:
Meteorology and Meteorologists

A. Pre-listening Activities

PREVIEW OF CONTENT

"Everyone talks about the weather, but nobody does anything about it," is a common expression, but is it really true that nobody is doing anything about the weather? This is definitely not true today. In this lecture, you will find out what scientists are doing about the weather.

The lecturer begins his talk by describing some of the contributions made by weather scientists. He goes on to talk about the United States National Weather Service's monitoring of weather conditions throughout the country. Specific examples of the Weather Service's information-gathering operation are given. The speaker then talks about the role weather satellites play in providing weather information and data to scientists. He finishes up by explaining how accurate weather information benefits us.

PREVIEW OF VOCABULARY

These are some of the vocabulary items contained in the lecture. Fill in each blank with one of the words listed. Use your dictionary to look up any items you are not familiar with.

make forecasts	meteorology	warn

1. Weather reports help to notify people of possible danger; they _____ of approaching storms.

2. To predict what the weather will be like in the future is to _____ about the weather.

3. _____ is the science of studying the weather.

satellite	network	launched

4. An object made by humans that is sent into outer space to collect weather information and data is called a weather_____ .

5. The weather satellite was sent into outer space and now revolves around the earth. It was _____ into space in 1959.

6. An interconnected group or system of weather stations is also called a _____ of weather stations.

CHECK YOUR ANSWERS.

PREVIEW OF SENTENCES

These are some of the sentences you will hear in the lecture. After having worked through the previous exercise, you should be familiar with the meanings of the italicized items.

1. Today *meteorology* is used to make people's lives safer and better.

2. Some meteorologists *make forecasts* about the weather.

3. Many weather forecasts help to *warn* people of approaching bad weather and storms.

4. The United States National Weather Service operates a *network* of weather stations throughout the United States.

5. In the year 1959, the United States *launched* its first weather *satellite*.

Symbols Used in the Note-Taking Model

Before you start the tape, take a minute to study the list of symbols used in the Note-Taking Model. You may wish to use some of these symbols when you take your notes on the lecture.

⟶	= provides	the ditto sign (") under a word indicates
+400	= more than 400	that the word above it is being repeated
%	= percent	$ = dollars
'59	= 1959	the – dash indicates that words have
&	= and	been omitted

B. Listening Activities

NOTE-TAKING MODEL

START THE TAPE.

You will now hear a lecture about the science of studying the weather, meteorology. As you listen, look at the Note-Taking Model. It is very brief. It is in outline form. It contains only the main ideas of the lecture and only the essential facts. Notice the symbols and abbreviations that have been used to save time in note-taking. After you have listened to the lecture once while looking at the model, you will listen to it a second time. Then, you will have a chance to take your own notes on the lecture. But for now, just listen and look at the Note-Taking Model.

The Weather: Meteorology and Meteorologists

meteor. — lives-safer & better
  ogists — study weather
   ” — observe ”
   ” — analyze ” info.
   ” — forecast ”
     ” — warn — approach. storms

USNWS — weather stations
  — 400+ ” — info. coll. & rec.
  — observ. — ev. hr. — day & night
  — issues 24 hr. forecasts
   ” 5 day ” } some 95% accur.
   ” 30 day ”

  ’59 — U.S. —weather satellite → weather info.
since ” — several ” ”→val. ” ” (world)

accur. forecasts — 1,000 lives & millions $ prop. dam.
meteor. — ” — safer & better

NOTE-TAKING EXERCISE

Now take out a piece of paper to take notes on, or use the space provided on this page, and listen to the lecture again. You should try to take notes similar to those in the Note-Taking Model. In other words, write down only the main ideas of the lecture and only the essential details. Write down all the numbers and dates you hear. Remember to use symbols and to abbreviate words.

To help you with the note-taking, some of the important information will be repeated for you. Before you begin, look at the *Word Guide*. These are examples of words that the lecturer might write on the blackboard before or during the lecture.

Word Guide

meteorology / meteorologists / the United States National Weather Service / weather satellite

_____

_____

_____

_____

_____

_____

_____

_____

_____

_____

_____

_____

MULTIPLE-CHOICE QUESTIONS

Now you are going to hear five questions about the information you heard in the lecture. Each question will be spoken two times, but it will not be written out for you. You must listen very carefully to each question. After you hear a question, read the four possible answers that are printed in your book. You should then check your notes to see which of the four choices is the *correct answer* to the question you heard. Mark your answer by putting an X next to the letter (a), (b), (c), or (d)—whichever is the best choice.

Listen to the following example.

You will hear the question: "What do *meteorologists* do?"

You will read in your book:

      (a) They observe the weather.
      (b) They analyze weather information.
      (c) They make weather forecasts.
X (d) All of the above.

After hearing the question, you should have looked at the notes you took and found some indication in them that meteorologists observe the weather, analyze weather information, and make weather forecasts; therefore, choice (d) is the correct answer. Now let's begin the test.

1. (a) exactly four hundred
   (b) fewer than four hundred
   (c) more than four hundred
   (d) all of the above

2. (a) five-hour
   (b) thirty-hour
   (c) twenty-four hour
   (d) all of the above

3. (a) 05%
   (b) 09%
   (c) 90%
   (d) 95%

4. (a) in the early 1950s
   (b) in the mid-1950s
   (c) in the late 1950s
   (d) none of the above

5. (a) They study about meteorology.
   (b) They talk about the weather.
   (c) They collect weather information.
   (d) They issue five-day weather forecasts.

Stop the tape and check your answers. Then continue working in your book. This is the end of the taped section of Lecture 2.

STOP THE TAPE.

C. Post-listening Activity

TRUE–FALSE STATEMENTS

In this exercise you will read ten statements about the information you learned in the lecture. First, read the statement. Then decide whether the statement is true or not. If it is true, place a T in the blank space next to the number of the statement you read. If it is not true, in other words, if it is false, place an F in the blank. You may want to check your notes before you make your choice. Read carefully.

1. ____ Nobody ever talks about the weather.

2. ____ Meteorology is used to make people's lives safer and better.

3. ____ Weather forecasts help to warn people of approaching good weather.

4. ____ The U.S. National Weather Service operates a system of stations in every country around the world.

5. ____ Weather observations are taken every sixty minutes at the U.S. National Weather Service.

6. ____ The Weather Service issues five-day as well as thirty-day weather forecasts.

7. ____ The United States launched its first satellite in 1959.

8. ____ Since 1959 no additional weather satellites have been sent into space.

9. ____ Weather satellites provide valuable weather information to meteorologists.

CHECK YOUR ANSWERS.

10. ____ Inaccurate weather forecasts can save thousands of lives and millions of dollars in property damage.

D. Follow-up Activities

WRITING EXERCISE

Read the following sentences from the lecture and reduce them to their key words. Write the sentence reduction on the blank line. Use symbols and abbreviations if possible.

For example: Meteorology is used to make people's lives safer and better.

Meteor → lives — safer & better

1. Some meteorologists observe the weather, others analyze weather information, and still others make forecasts about the weather.

   _____

2. The United States Weather Service has more than 400 weather stations where information about the weather is collected and recorded.

   _____

3. The Weather Service issues twenty-four-hour weather forecasts. It also issues five-day forecasts and even thirty-day forecasts.

   _____

4. In the year 1959, the United States launched its first weather satellite.

   _____

5. Accurate weather forecasts can save thousands of lives and millions of dollars in property damage.

   _____

TOPICS FOR DISCUSSION OR WRITING

1. Does your country have a national weather service? How does it operate?

2. How can a weather satellite be used to help save thousands of lives and millions of dollars in property damage?

3. You are planning to go on a camping trip or a picnic in the mountains this coming weekend. When and how will you find out what the weather will be like on the weekend?

4. Describe an experience you had when you were caught in a sudden storm. Where were you when the storm struck? Who was with you? What kind of storm was it? How long did the storm last? What did you do during the storm? What happened when the storm ended? Did you listen to the weather forecast the morning of the storm?

Thirty-Day Weather Report for the Continental United States

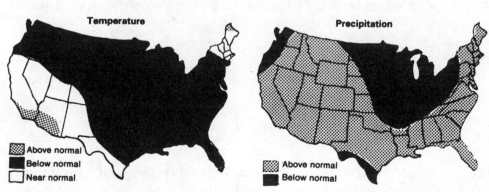

Answer the following questions by referring to the Thirty-Day Weather Report.

1. Which states will have warmer than usual temperatures?

2. Will the state of Florida have warmer or cooler than usual temperatures?

3. Will the Northeast of the country receive more or less than usual rainfall?

4. Will the northwestern tip of California receive a greater or lesser amount of precipitation than it normally does?

5. Will temperatures be above or below normal in the American Midwest?

6. Will the U.S. experience colder and wetter weather or warmer and drier during this 30-day period?

7. Describe the outlook for the Northern Midwest.

8. What is the temperature forecast for the Northwest of the country?

The Grand Canyon: One of Nature's Finest Monuments

A. Pre-listening Activities

PREVIEW OF CONTENT

The following lecture is about the Grand Canyon National Park, located in the southwestern part of the United States, in northern Arizona.

The lecturer begins by describing the Canyon's location, dimensions, and climate variations. She then touches upon the geology of the area and the plant and animal life found in the Grand Canyon Park. After this, she mentions the discovery of the Canyon by Spanish soldiers, and then she talks about the various tribes of Native Americans who presently inhabit the area around the Canyon. The lecture ends with her citing the reason the president of the United States decided to establish the area as a national park. He wished to protect the plants and animals of the area, and to provide people with a view of one of Nature's finest monuments to be found in the United States.

PREVIEW OF VOCABULARY

These are some of the vocabulary items contained in the lecture. Fill in each blank with one of the words listed. Use your dictionary to look up any items you are not familiar with.

---

fossils   Hopi   Navajo   Havasupai

---

1. The remains of a plant or animal preserved in the earth from ages past are called _____ .

2. The names of three Indian tribes or groups that live in the Grand Canyon area are _____ , _____ , and _____ .

---

rim   spectacular   expedition   gorge

---

3. A journey or trip to explore an area or region is referred to as an _____ .

4. The outer edge or border of the Grand Canyon is known as its _____ .

5. The Grand Canyon is sensational: it is really _____ .

6. A very large, narrow, and deep valley with high walls is a _____ .

mammals	abundant	reservations	geologic

7. _____ change is change that results from the history of the earth as seen in the rocks and stones of an area.

8. Public lands that have been set aside for the Indians to live on and to use are designated as _____ .

9. Animals that feed their babies with milk are classified as _____ .

10. There is plentiful plant life in the Canyon; there is also _____ animal life in the area.

CHECK YOUR ANSWERS.

PREVIEW OF SENTENCES

These are some of the sentences you will hear in the lecture. After having worked through the previous exercise, you should be familiar with the meanings of the italicized items.

1. The Grand Canyon is a *spectacular* sight to see.

2. The Grand Canyon is really a huge *gorge* which was cut by the Colorado River.

3. The north *rim* of the Grand Canyon is 1,000 feet higher than the south *rim*.

4. The Grand Canyon walls hold a long record of *geologic* change.

5. You can see many plant and animal *fossils* in the Grand Canyon rock walls.

6. Plant and animal life in the Canyon is quite *abundant* and varied.

7. There are about sixty-seven species or varieties of *mammals* in the Grand Canyon area.

8. The first Europeans to see the Grand Canyon were Spaniards. They were members of Coronado's *expedition* of 1540.

9. The *Navajo*, the *Hopi*, and the *Havasupai* live on *reservations* in the Grand Canyon area.

Symbols Used in the Note-Taking Model

Before you start the tape, study the four symbols used in the Note-Taking Model.

5,000'	five thousand feet	−10	less than 10
26"	twenty-six inches	⟶	in order to

B. Listening Activities

NOTE-TAKING MODEL

Now you will hear the lecture. As you listen to it, look at the note-taking model. It is brief. It is in outline form. It contains only the main ideas of the lecture and only the essential details. After you have listened to the lecture once while looking at the model, you will listen to it again. Then, you will take your own notes on the lecture. For now, just listen and look at the model.

START THE TAPE.

The Grand Canyon: One of Nature's Finest Monuments

G.C.   — Colo. R. — 1,000s visit no. AZ

dimen.   217 mi.   l.
              +1   "   d.
              4—18 mi.   w.
              5,000—10,000' h.
              no. rim — 1,000' higher   — so. rim
              "   "   colder than   "   "

rain   "   "   = 26" rain   — "   " 16" rain
              Can. fl. = -10"   "

Can. walls   — Colo. R. = geo. change — pl. & anim. fossils
              — 1,000 plants

p. & anim.   + 200 birds
              67 mammals

1st Europ.   — see G.C.   — Sp.   — Coronado   — 1540   — by Hopi Ind.

Today   Navajo   — 15,000,000 acre res.   — east   — center

              — Hopi   — 631,000   "   "
              — 200 Havasupai — 518   "   "   — near

'19   — Pres. Wilson estab. G.C. Nat. Park →prot. land & wildlife

Today   — Amer. & for. visit G.C.

NOTE-TAKING EXERCISE

Now take out a piece of paper for notes or use the blank space on this page and listen to the lecture again. As you listen, take your own notes on the lecture. You should try to take notes similar to those found in the model. Be brief. Use outline form. Use symbols and abbreviations. Write down only the main points of the lecture and only the essential details.

To help you with the note-taking, some of the important information will be repeated for you, but before you begin, look at the *Word Guide*. These are examples of words that the lecturer might write on the blackboard before or during the lecture.

Word Guide:

The Grand Canyon / Colorado River / geologic change / Spaniards / Coronado / Hopi / Navajo / Havasupai / President Woodrow Wilson

MULTIPLE-CHOICE QUESTIONS

Now you are going to hear ten questions about the information you heard in the lecture. Each question will be spoken two times, but it will not be written out for you. You must listen very carefully to each question. After you hear a question, read the four possible answers which are printed in your book. You should then check your notes and decide which of the four choices *best answers* the question you have heard. Mark your answer by putting an X next to the letter (a), (b), (c), or (d)—whichever is the correct choice.

Listen to the following example:

You will hear: "In what part of Arizona is the Grand Canyon located?"

You will read in your book: in _____ Arizona.

X (a) northern
(b) southern
(c) eastern
(d) western

You should have looked at the notes you took on the lecture and found an abbreviation or other indication that the Grand Canyon is located in northern Arizona; therefore, choice (a) is the correct answer.

1. (a) 207
   (b) 217
   (c) 270
   (d) none of the above

2. (a) 4
   (b) 18
   (c) neither of the above
   (d) both of the above

3. (a) 10
   (b) 16
   (c) 20
   (d) 26

4. (a) animals
   (b) fossils
   (c) mammals
   (d) plants

5. (a) 67
   (b) 200
   (c) 2,000
   (d) none of the above

6. (a) 67
   (b) 133
   (c) 200
   (d) 1,000

7. (a) 1415
   (b) 1450
   (c) 1514
   (d) 1540

8. (a) Hopi
   (b) Navajo
   (c) Papago
   (d) Havasupai

9. (a) fifteen million   10. (a) two hundred
   (b) five hundred eighteen   (b) five hundred eighteen
   (c) six hundred thirteen   (c) six hundred thousand
      thousand   (d) fifteen million
   (d) none of the above

If you took sufficient, organized notes, you should have been able to locate the answers to the questions in your notes.

STOP THE TAPE.

Stop the tape and check your answers. Then continue with the written exercises. This is the end of the taped section of Lecture 3.

C. Post-listening Activities

TRUE–FALSE STATEMENTS

In this exercise, you will read twelve statements about the Grand Canyon. First read the statement carefully. After checking your notes, decide whether the statement is true or false. If it is true, place a T in the blank space next to the number of the statement. If it is false, place an F in the blank. Remember to use your notes to help you answer the questions.

1.____ The Grand Canyon's narrow valley is 207 miles long.

2.____ The Canyon is from four to eighteen miles deep.

3.____ The Canyon's south rim is 1,000 feet lower than its north rim.

4.____ The average amount of rainfall for the south rim of the Canyon is about twenty-six inches.

5.____ On the floor of the Canyon no more than ten inches of rain fall in a year.

6.____ There is a long record of geographic change in the walls of the Grand Canyon.

7.____ At least sixty-seven kinds of animals that feed their babies with milk live in the Grand Canyon Park.

8.____ The first Europeans to see the Grand Canyon were guided to it by the Navajo Indians.

9. ___ White men first saw the Grand Canyon in the fifteenth century.

10. ___ Today the Hopi Indians live on a 631,000-acre reservation.

11. ___ The Hopi have more land than the Havasupai Indians do.

12. ___ President Woodrow Wilson established the Grand Canyon National Park in the mid-twentieth century.

CHECK YOUR ANSWERS.

WRITING EXERCISE

In this exercise you are to reconstruct a grammatical English sentence from a string of words, abbreviations, numbers, and symbols. This is just the reverse of reducing a complete sentence to its note-taking form. You may use the lecture script to help you if necessary.

For example: The notes: gorge = 217 mi. l. & + 1 mi. d.   can be rewritten as:

The gorge is 217 miles long and more than 1 mile deep.

1. area ar. Canyon = 5,000' & 10,000' h.

   _____

2. no. rim – Canyon – 1,000' higher – so. rim

   _____

3. G.C. Park = 1,000 plants & + 200 species birds

   _____

4. '19 Pres. W. Wilson estab. G.C. Nat. Park ⟶ prot. anim. & land

   _____

5. 1st Europ. – see G.C. – Spaniards (Coronado's exped.)

   _____

D. Follow-up Activity

TOPICS FOR DISCUSSION OR WRITING

1. The Grand Canyon may be Nature's Finest Monument in the United States, but what is Nature's Finest Monument in your country? Describe the natural wonder. Where is it located? What are its dimensions?

2. Do you feel that the establishment of National Parks would help to protect and preserve the wild animals and the virgin land in your country?

3. What is your country presently doing to protect and preserve its natural wonders from exploitation and overdevelopment?

4. Has the industrial development of your country ruined some of its beautiful natural wonders and land? Explain what has happened, giving specific examples of areas in your country that have suffered from industrial pollution, overcrowding, overbuilding, and so forth.

Japan: Industrial Giant of the Far East

A. Pre-listening Activities

PREVIEW OF CONTENT

Since World War II, the small country of Japan has become one of the world's leading industrial nations. It enjoys the highest standard of living in all Asia today. Japan has, however, been plagued by certain economic and environmental problems since the war's end. Over-crowding of her cities is one of these problems. A scarcity of natural resources is another, which is a threat to her very economic stability. Industrial pollution and inflation trouble Japan today as, indeed, they do every major industrial nation in the world. And yet, in spite of these problems, art, culture, learning, and sports flourish in this ancient, but modern country.

The lecturer begins his talk about Japan by saying a few words about the size, location, climate, and population of the country. He then discusses the problems that plague Japan today. After this, he turns to talking about the Japanese people's respect for art, learning, and education, and their knack for combining the Oriental and Western ways of life into their lifestyle. He ends up by touching upon how the Japanese spend their free time enjoying sports and travel.

PREVIEW OF VOCABULARY

Fill in each blank with one of the words listed. Use your dictionary to check the meaning of an item you are not familiar with.

leisure time	raw materials	literacy	ceramics

1. Time free from work or duties is _____ .

2. _____ is the ability to read and write.

3. The art of making pots and dishes from clay which is first shaped and later hardened by heat is the art of making _____ .

4. Materials that can be manufactured or prepared to be made more useful to man are referred to as _____ .

wrestling	enterprising	cite	threaten

5. The Japanese are an energetic people. They are ready to try new, important, and difficult plans. You might say they are an _____ people.

6. Tropical storms are a source of danger to Japan during the fall. They _____ Japan during the harvest season.

7. A sport in which two persons struggle hand to hand, trying to throw or force each other to the ground, is called _____ .

8. I want to give you an example of a problem facing Japan today. I'll _____ the problem of industrial pollution.

---

luxury   inflation   prosperity   population density

---

9. That which is not a basic necessity in life—a basic necessity like food, water, and shelter—might be termed a _____ by some people.

10. The substantial and continuous rise in the price of goods is referred to as _____ .

11. The _____ of Japan is based on the average number of persons living in a definite area, usually a square mile area.

12. Japan's economic growth and development have resulted in _____ for the country. Japan has become a rich country as a result of this growth and development.

CHECK YOUR ANSWERS.

PREVIEW OF SENTENCES

These are some of the sentences you will hear in the lecture. After having worked through the Preview of Vocabulary, you should be familiar with the meaning of the italicized words.

1. Tropical storms often *threaten* Japan during the fall. That's, of course, during the harvest season.

2. The average *population density* of Japan is about 678 persons per square mile.

3. Let me *cite* a few other problems facing Japan today.

4. Japan must import most of its minerals. Japan must also import large quantities of food and *raw materials.*

5. Japan's amazing economic growth has brought problems as well as *prosperity* to the country.

6. Industrial pollution and *inflation* are major problems for Japan today.

7. To the Japanese, *literacy* is a necessity rather than a *luxury*; 95 percent of the Japanese people are *literate.* They're able to read and write.

8. The Japanese often express their love of beauty in the creation and enjoyment of beautiful art, sculpture, *ceramics,* music, and theatre productions.

9. The Japanese work very hard. They are an industrious, hard-working, and *enterprising* people.

10. Although they are very hard-working, the Japanese still manage to enjoy their *leisure time.*

11. The Japanese really enjoy sports, such as soccer, swimming, judo, *wrestling,* karate, and baseball.

B. Listening Activities

NOTE-TAKING MODEL

START THE TAPE.

You are going to hear a lecture about Japan. As you listen, look at the Note-Taking Model. It is brief. It is in outline form. It contains only the main ideas of the lecture and only the necessary facts. You will notice that symbols and abbreviations have been used to save note-taking time. After you have listened to the lecture once while looking at the model, you will hear it for a second time. You will then have to take your own notes on the information you hear. For now, just listen and look at the Note-Taking Model.

Japan: Industrial Giant of the Far East

Japan   — Pac. O. (4 + 3,000 islands) $\updownarrow$ 1,300 mi.

climate   hot + hum. — S.
               cold + wet —W.
               typhoons   — F.   — harvest

pop.   — 110½ m.   — pop. den. = 678/sq. mi.
                                         57 "   " U.S.

  probs.   2/3 pop.   — cities
               1/3 "   — suburbs
               Tokyo   — most den. pop.   — world — 11.5 m.

resources   — var.   — min. — # small (Au, Cu, Ag, etc.)
               import food & raw mat.
               export prod. — man. (TV, cars, etc.)
               since W W II — chief ind. & man. country
                            — highest stand. liv. — Asia
                            — problems (ind. poll. & infl.)

education   — literacy   — nec. — 95%
                            — school — 9 yrs.
                                      6 " elem.
                                      3 " jr. h.s.
                                      sr. h.s. & univ.   — if pass diff.
                                                            entr. exam.

culture   — learning trad. & beauty;
               art sculp. ceram. mus. theat. prod.

way of life   — comb. Japnse & Western
               food, books, cloth. music
               Orient. & West. at home — Tokyo

people   — ind. hardwork. enterp. → growth — econ.
               enjoy leisure
               sports (soccer swimm. judo wrestl. karate baseball)
               vac. trips home & abroad

NOTE-TAKING EXERCISE

Now listen to the lecture again. As you listen, take notes on the information you hear. You should try to take notes that are similar to those in the Note-Taking Model. Remember, write down only the words that carry information such as facts and figures. It is not necessary to write down prepositions or articles. Of course, you should use abbreviations and symbols.

To assist you with the note-taking, some of the important information will be repeated for you. Before you begin, look at the *Word Guide*. These are samples of words that the lecturer might write on the blackboard before or during his lecture.

Word Guide

Pacific Ocean / typhoons / Asia / Tokyo / Oriental / Western / judo / wrestling / karate

_____

_____

_____

_____

_____

_____

_____

_____

_____

_____

_____

_____

_____

_____

_____

_____

_____

_____

_____

_____

_____

_____

_____

_____

_____

_____

_____

_____

_____

_____

_____

_____

MULTIPLE-CHOICE QUESTIONS

Now you are going to hear ten questions about Japan. Each of the questions will be spoken two times, but the questions will not be written out for you. Listen carefully to each question. After hearing the question, read the four possible answers that are printed in your book. You should then check your notes to see which of the four choices is the *correct answer* to the question you hear. Mark your answer by putting an X next to the letter (a), (b), (c), or (d)—whichever is the best choice.

Listen to the following example:

You will hear the question: "How many islands make up the country of Japan?"

You will read in your book:

> (a) three thousand
> (b) three thousand four
> (c) three thousand forty
> X (d) none of the above

You should have checked your notes and found that four main islands and *more than* three thousand small ones make up the country of Japan; therefore, choice (d) is the correct answer.

Are you ready to begin the test?

1. (a) three hundred
   (b) one thousand
   (c) one thousand three hundred
   (d) three thousand one hundred

2. (a) 10,000,000
   (b) 110,000,000
   (c) 110,500,000
   (d) none of the above

3. (a) 57
   (b) 87
   (c) 621
   (d) 687

4. (a) 10
   (b) 25
   (c) 33 1/3
   (d) 66 2/3

5. (a) materials
   (b) raw materials
   (c) products they grow
   (d) products they manufacture

6. (a) inflation
   (b) prosperity
   (c) industrial pollution
   (d) all of the above

7. (a) 3
   (b) 6
   (c) 9
   (d) 12

8. in their choice of
   (a) food
   (b) books
   (c) clothing
   (d) all of the above

9. (a) European
   (b) Oriental
   (c) American
   (d) all of the above

10. (a) judo
    (b) karate
    (c) baseball
    (d) hockey

Check your answers. Then continue working in your book. This is the end of the taped section of Lecture 4.

STOP THE TAPE.

C. Post-listening Activity

TRUE-FALSE STATEMENTS

Here are ten statements about the information presented in the lecture. First read the statement. Then decide whether the statement is true or false. If it is true, place a T in the blank space next to the number of the statement you read. If it is false, place an F in the blank. Of course, you should check your notes before making your choice.

1. ____ Japan is about 1,300 miles wide.

2. ____ No other country in Asia has as large an urban population as Japan.

3. ____ Japan's amazing economic and industrial growth has brought nothing but prosperity to the country.

4. ____ A smaller proportion of Japanese dwell in the rural areas than in the urban areas.

5. ____ Tokyo is the most densely-populated city in the world.

6. ____ Japan has a large variety and quantity of minerals.

7. ____ The Japanese people enjoy the highest standard of living in the world.

8. ____ Every Japanese student is required to attend both junior and senior high school.

9. ____ Respect for tradition and learning have always been very important to the Japanese.

10. ____ The recent growth of the Japanese economy reflects the enterprise and industriousness of the Japanese people.

CHECK YOUR ANSWERS.

D. Follow-up Activities

TOPICS FOR DISCUSSION OR WRITING

1. Industrial pollution and inflation are two of the major problems facing Japan today. Specify two or three of the major problems facing your country today, and describe how they are affecting the lives of your countrymen. Discuss several possible methods of solving these problems.

2. Japan has experienced and tolerated a tremendous amount of "Americanization" since World War II. This infusion of American culture and ideology has impacted upon Japan's social, political, and commercial systems. Has there been any similar "foreign" influence that has brought about tremendous changes in the social, political, or commercial systems of your country? Discuss the impact upon your country of a major foreign influence. Discuss the advantages and the disadvantages brought by this foreign influence.

3. Respect for tradition is a Japanese characteristic. Compare and contrast the concept of respect for tradition in your country and (a) Japan, or (b) the United States.

4. "Japan would be a different country today if she had won World War II." Elaborate upon this theme.

Kuwait:
Pipeline of the Middle East

كويت

A. Pre-listening Activities

PREVIEW OF CONTENT

Since the discovery of oil, many Arab countries have become rich and powerful states. In many ways, the small country of Kuwait is representative of all the developing Arab nations. The discovery of oil has had an enormous impact on the economic, social, and, indirectly, the political structure of the country. The country has been turned into a modern, working welfare state by its rulers.

Oil, first exported in the late forties, is the basis of the country's economy. It pays for free medical care, education, and social security. And, Kuwaitis are not required to pay any personal income tax for these services and benefits.

The lecturer starts off with the geography and climate of the country. He then switches to the impact of the discovery of oil on the economic and social order. He cites an influx of immigrants from all over the world into the country to take advantage of the growth and modernization of the country. Kuwait is a country in which the majority of the population is non-Kuwaiti. The lecturer lists some of the countries the immigrants have come from. Then he briefly mentions something about the modernization that has taken place in the country's capital, Kuwait City. He finishes up by giving an overview of the political structure of the Kuwaiti government.

PREVIEW OF VOCABULARY

Fill in each blank with one of the items listed. Use your dictionary to check the meaning of an item you are not familiar with.

---

sheikh   dynasty   emir   prosperous

---

1. A continuation of rulers from the same family is a
   _____ .

2. The two terms that refer to an Arab chief, leader, or prince are
   _____ and _____ .

3. The people of Kuwait are economically well off. They are
   _____ .

---

constitutional monarchy   per capita   Bedouin nomads

---

4. The _____ are the Arab wanderers of the desert who constantly move from one place to another.

5. A kingdom regulated or ruled according to a constitution is a
   _____ .

6.   When we talk of the amount of money earned by each person per year in Kuwait, we are referring to the country's income _____ .

---

executive power   reserves   income tax

---

7.   The extra supplies of oil that have been set aside for future use are the petroleum _____ of the country.

8.   Kuwaitis do not have to pay any personal _____ . There is no charge placed on the money they earn by the government to provide the social services they enjoy.

9.   The government power to put laws into effect is exercised by the Emir. He exercises this _____ through a Prime Minister, a Council, and a National Assembly.

CHECK YOUR ANSWERS.

PREVIEW OF SENTENCES

---

1.   Before 1938 Kuwait was a little-known Arab state which was ruled by an Arab *sheikh.*

2.   Kuwait has approximately 15 percent of the world's known petroleum *reserves.*

3.   In terms of national income *per capita,* Kuwait is one of the world's richest nations.

4.   Kuwait's rulers have turned the country into a *prosperous* welfare state.

5.   Kuwaitis do not have to pay any personal *income tax* for the social services, such as schooling and health care.

6.   *Bedouin nomads* who lived outside the town raised camels, goats, and sheep.

7.   Kuwait is a *constitutional monarchy* whose head of state is the *Emir.*

8. The *Sabah dynasty* has ruled Kuwait for over 200 years. It was founded in 1756.

9. The Emir exercises *executive power* through a Prime Minister, a Council, and a National Assembly.

B. Listening Activities

NOTE-TAKING MODEL

START THE TAPE.

   You are going to hear a lecture about Kuwait. As you listen, look at the Note-Taking Model. It is brief. It is in outline form. It contains only the main ideas of the lecture and only the necessary facts. You will notice that symbols and abbreviations have been used to save note-taking time. After you have listened to the lecture once while looking at the Model, you will hear it for a second time. You will then have to take your own notes on the information you hear. For now, just listen and look at the Note-Taking Model.

Kuwait: Pipeline of the Middle East

Kuwait   — sm. — rich
       — pop. — +1 mil.
       — north end — Arab. Gulf (Persian)
       — area — 8,000 sq. mi. (2 m. hectares)
       — climate   — summer   — $124°$ F = $51.1°$ C
                     — winter   — $50° - 60°$ F = $10° - 15.5°$ C

oil disc.   — '38 — little known   — ruled by sheikh
       — now — a leading oil prod.
                — 15%   " reserves
       — since oil   — pros. welf. st.:
                — free ed., health & soc. services
                — no income tax
                — 1 of wealthiest (per capita) — $11,431
                                         (3,184 Dinars)
                — high lit. (Univ. '66) many students abroad
                (st. exp.)

pop.   — 99% Moslem (-½ citizens)
       —   "   immigrants — Egy. Syr. Leb. Sud. Oman Ind.
       Pak. Iran
       — 1% non Moslem — Oil companies — Eur. Am.

until oil disc.   — lived trad. style
                        — inside town — mud houses
                        — outside ”   — Bedouins — raise camels, goats, sheep
                        — old town gone — K.C.

6/19/61   — indep.

today   — const. mon. — head = Emir
                        —   ” chosen for life (Sabah)
                        — Sabah dyn. = +200 yrs. (1756)
                        — Emir = exec. power + P.M. + Council (15) + N.A. (50 mem
                                           $\simeq$ 4 yrs.)
                                       ” el. by citiz.

                        — only citizens vote
                        — all Ks benefit

NOTE-TAKING EXERCISE

Now listen to the lecture again. As you listen, take notes on the information you hear. You may want to take notes similar to those in the Note-Taking Model. Remember, write down only the words that carry information such as dates and statistics. It is not necessary to write down prepositions or articles. Of course, you should use abbreviations and symbols.

To assist you with the note-taking, some of the important information will be repeated for you. Before you begin, look at the *Word Guide.* These are samples of words that the lecturer might write on the blackboard before or during his lecture.

Word Guide

Kuwait / The Arabian Gulf / The Persian Gulf / Fahrenheit / Centigrade / Celsius / sheikh / dinar / Moslems / Egypt / Syria / Lebanon / The Sudan / Oman / Indians / Pakistanis / Iranians / Europeans / Americans / Bedouin nomads / Emir / Sabah

_____

_____

_____

_____

_____

_____

_____

_____

_____

_____

_____

_____

MULTIPLE-CHOICE QUESTIONS

You will now hear eleven questions about Kuwait. Each question will be spoken two times, but it will not be written out for you. After you hear a question, read the four possible answers that are printed in your book. Check the notes you took on the lecture and decide which of the four choices *best answers* the question you have heard. Mark your answer by putting an X next to the letter (a), (b), (c), or (d)—whichever is the best choice.

For example:

You will hear the question: "What is the land area of the country of Kuwait?"

You will read in your book:

> X (a) eight thousand square miles
> (b) two million square miles
> (c) eight thousand hectares
> (d) none of the above

After checking your notes, you should have decided that choice (a) is the correct answer since it was stated in the lecture that the land area of Kuwait is about eight thousand square miles or two million hectares.

Are you ready for the first question? It's a bit tricky, so be careful.

1. (a) 50°
   (b) 60°
   (c) 74°
   (d) 124°

2. (a) 124° to 51.1° Celsius
   (b) 10° to 15.5° Celsius
   (c) 124° to 50° Fahrenheit
   (d) 50° to 10° Fahrenheit

3. (a) 1908
   (b) 1930
   (c) 1938
   (d) 1966

4. (a) 1/3
   (b) 1/4
   (c) 1/10
   (d) 3/20

5. approximately
   (a) $1.00
   (b) $3.59
   (c) $5.39
   (d) $9.33

6. (a) 28 years
   (b) 29 years
   (c) 30 years
   (d) none of the above

7. (a) 01%
   (b) 19%
   (c) 99%
   (d) none of the above

8. (a) Oman
   (b) Pakistan
   (c) Syria
   (d) Yemen

9. (a) June, 1916
   (b) July, 1961
   (c) June, 1960
   (d) none of the above

11. (a) 15 members
    (b) 35 members
    (c) 50 members
    (d) none of the above

10. (a) fewer than a hundred years
    (b) more than two hundred years
    (c) more than three hundred years
    (d) all of the above

Check your answers. Then continue working in your book. This is the end of the taped section of Lecture 5.

STOP THE TAPE.

C. Post-listening Activity

TRUE–FALSE STATEMENTS

In this exercise, you are given eleven statements about Kuwait. First read the statement. Then decide whether the statement is accurate or inaccurate according to the information presented by the lecturer. If the statement is true, place a T in the blank space next to the number of the statement. If it is false, place an F next to the number of the statement. You should, of course, use your notes to help you determine the accuracy or inaccuracy of the statements.

1. ____ The Arabian Gulf and the Persian Gulf are two different bodies of water.

2. ____ On the Fahrenheit scale, temperatures range between 15.5° and 10° during the winter days.

3. ____ Kuwait was ruled by an Arab sheikh even before oil was discovered there.

4. ____ Kuwaitis are heavily taxed to provide for the social services the country provides its citizens.

5. ____ Many Kuwaiti students are on government scholarships at foreign universities.

6. ____ Fewer than half of the inhabitants of Kuwait take a part in the country's electoral process.

7. ____ The oil companies have attracted many foreigners into Kuwait.

8. ____ Bedouin nomads used to live in the old walled town of Kuwait.

9. ____ Kuwait's system of government bears certain similarities to Great Britain's system.

10. ____ The Emir of Kuwait is elected for life by a majority of the Kuwaiti people.

11. ____ Only the citizens of Kuwait can vote, but all the people who live and work in the country benefit from the country's social services.

CHECK YOUR ANSWERS.

D. Follow-up Activities

TOPICS FOR DISCUSSION OR WRITING

1. List the advantages Kuwaitis enjoy as citizens of a prosperous welfare state. You may use the lecture script to formulate your answer. Then list the advantages you enjoy as a citizen of your country.

2. In the country of Kuwait, there are many immigrant groups. Are there any immigrant groups in your native country? Describe where they are from; why they are in your country; what they do to earn a living. Discuss the benefits and problems they present for your country.

3. Compare and contrast your country and Kuwait in terms of the size of the country, the climate, the religion, the political system, the major natural resource, and the welfare benefits. Include any other relevant categories of comparison or contrast in your answer.

Languages in Conflict:
Irish and English

A. Pre-listening Activities

PREVIEW OF CONTENT

In the small country of Ireland, two languages are used by the people: Irish, which is the native language, and English, which is the language that was brought to Ireland by the invading armies of England in the twelfth century. While English is the dominant language of the country today, some Irishmen have struggled to keep alive their national language. In this lecture, you will learn something about the historic struggle and conflict between Ireland's two languages: Irish and English.

The lecturer opens up his presentation by giving some information about the location, size, and population of the tiny country. He also alludes to the political and national division that exists between Northern Ireland, which is part of the British Commonwealth, and the Republic of Ireland, which is not.

The rest of the lecture is organized chronologically. First, mention is made of Ireland's cultural importance in the early Middle Ages. After this, the lecturer jumps ahead to the Norman-English invasion of the country in the 1100s. In the sixteenth century, the country was subjugated and brought under English domination. Hard times followed up through the eighteenth and nineteenth centuries. Failure of the potato crop due to poor weather conditions brought death from hunger to the population and forced a million Irishmen to leave their homeland for the U.S., Canada, and other countries. The lecturer notes that in the nineteenth century, use of the native language declined drastically, with only a small proportion of the Irish people speaking the national language. An effort was made, however, in the early twentieth century to reestablish use of the national language in the country. The speaker will give specific examples of these attempts and will finish up his presentation with the remark that, perhaps because of these measures, Ireland's national language will continue to exist in that small country.

PREVIEW OF VOCABULARY

Fill in each blank with the appropriate item.

---

exploitation   barbarians   The Norman-English

---

1. Invaders of the ancient Roman Empire, whose way of life is considered primitive, are known as _____ .

2. _____ is the unfair use of someone or some country for personal or national profit.

3. _____ were the French people who conquered the island of Ireland in the twelfth century—in the 1100s.

| persecution | coffin | Great Potato Famine | clergy |

4. The religious officials who conduct Christian services are referred to as the _____ .

5. A _____ is a box or case in which a dead body is placed.

6. _____ is the term that describes the refusal to permit people to act and believe as they want to.

7. The period of great hunger and death in Ireland resulting from the failure of the potato crop, which was the major source of food for the Irish, is termed the _____ .

| starvation | decree | extinction | lack |

8. _____ entails causing something to be destroyed or done away with.

9. To be without or to need is to _____ that which is needed.

10. To issue an order which must be obeyed is to _____ something.

11. Death from hunger is _____ .

CHECK YOUR ANSWERS.

PREVIEW OF SENTENCES

These are some of the sentences you will hear in the lecture:

1. When the *barbarians* conquered the continent of Europe, it was Ireland that kept alive Western culture and learning.

2. In the twelfth century—that is to say in the 1100s—the *Norman-English* conquest of Ireland began.

3. Throughout the eighteenth century—that is, throughout the 1700s—the Irish suffered from economic *exploitation* and political and religious *persecution*.

4. In the four years after the potato crop failure, more than one million people died of *starvation*.

5. The ships were called "floating *coffins*" because of the large number of people who died on board during the journey.

6. The *Great Potato Famine* occurred in 1847.

7. English was the language of the politicians, the *clergy,* and the landlords.

8. The government *decreed* that knowledge of the Irish language was required for all elementary school teachers.

9. By 1949 only 8.2 percent of the teachers *lacked* a certificate to teach Irish to the school children.

10. The near-*extinction* of a language spoken for more than two thousand years has, perhaps, been slowed down, or even stopped altogether.

B. Listening Activities

NOTE-TAKING MODEL

START THE TAPE.

Let's get ready to hear a lecture about the Republic of Ireland and the preservation of its national language. While you listen to the lecture, you should be looking at the Note-Taking Model, which is brief, which is in outline form, and which contains only the necessary facts and information contained in the lecture. Notice that the lecture information has been greatly condensed or reduced to its most important, information-carrying words. Of course, after you have listened to the lecture once while looking at the Note-Taking Model, you will be expected to take your own notes on the lecture. For now, just listen and look at the model.

Languages in Conflict: Irish and English

Rep. of Ire.	— nw. Eur.
	— land area = 26,600 sq. mi.
	— pop. = 3 m.
No. Ire.	— Br. Commonwealth — sep. — Rep. of Ire.
Mid. Ages	— 5th and 6th c. = prin. cult. center Eur.
	— kept alive — West. cult. & learn.
	— when barbs. conqd.
12th c.	— (late 1100s) — Norm. Eng. conquest began
	” controlled Ire.
16th c.	— lands taken — given to Eng. + Scot. settlers
	— rebellions put down
18th c.	— (1700s) — econ. exploit. + pol. & rel. persec.
	— people — poverty
late 1840s	— potato crop failed ← bad weather — (pot. prin. food)
1830s	— pop. = 9 m.
4 yrs. later	= +1 m. died — starv.
	= +1½ m. left — Canada, U.S., others — floating coffins
early 19th c.	— Irish spoken everywhere — Ire.
after GPF - 1847	— ” dec./Eng. replaced Irish
- 1870	— only 20% spoke nat. lang.
lat. ½ 19th c.	— (1850-1900) — Eng. lang. of schools, pol. clergy, &
	landlords
	— Eng. — lang. of rulers — Irish — lang. of ruled
1922	— self-gov’t.
’49	— free repub. → movement → Irish nat. lang.
	— know Irish — elem. teachers
by ’49	— only 8.2% — no certific. — teach Irish — children
today	— Irish — req. subj. coll. matric. since 1913 (except
	Trinity — Dublin)
	— gov’t. papers — 2 lang
	—newspapers — Irish
	— pol. must speak Irish
	— ext. lang. spoken + 2,000 yrs. — slowed, stopped

NOTE-TAKING EXERCISE

This time listen to the lecture and take your own concise notes on the information you hear about Ireland and its language. Remember that your notes should contain only the important facts found in the lecture. Some of these facts and figures will be repeated for you to make sure you have enough time to get them down. Are you ready to begin?

Word Guide

the Republic of Ireland / Europe / Northern Ireland / England / the Middle Ages / Norman-English / Scottish / Irish / the Great Potato Famine / Trinity College / Dublin

_____

_____

_____

_____

_____

_____

_____

_____

_____

_____

_____

_____

_____

_____

MULTIPLE-CHOICE QUESTIONS

You are going to hear twelve questions about the lecture. Each question will be spoken two times, but it will not be written out for you. After hearing a question, you should read the four possible choices that are printed in your book. You should then check your notes and decide which of the four possible choices is the *best answer* to the question you have heard. You will then mark your answer by putting an X next to the letter (a), (b), (c), or (d)—whichever is the correct choice.

For example:

You will hear: "When did the Norman-English conquest of Ireland begin?"

You will read in your book:

in the
(a) 1000s
X (b) 1100s
(c) 1200s
(d) 1600s

You should have checked the notes you took on the lecture after hearing the question, and you should have decided that the Norman-English conquest of Ireland began in the twelfth century, in other words in the 1100s. O.K., let's get on with the questions.

1. a little less than:
   (a) 1,000,000
   (b) 1,500,000
   (c) 3,000,000
   (d) 9,000,000

2. in the
   (a) 5th century
   (b) 6th century
   (c) both (a) and (b)
   (d) neither (a) nor (b)

3. in the
   (a) 13th century
   (b) 14th century
   (c) 15th century
   (d) 16th century

4. (a) economic exploitation
   (b) political persecution
   (c) religious persecution
   (d) all of the above

5. (a) 1,000,000 people starved to death
   (b) 1,500,000 people left England for Ireland
   (c) 9,000,000 people left Ireland on floating coffins
   (d) none of the above

6. in
   (a) 1807
   (b) 1840
   (c) 1847
   (d) 1870

7. during the
   (a) first half of the 18th century
   (b) latter half of the 18th century
   (c) first half of the 19th century
   (d) latter half of the 19th century

8. in
   (a) 1922
   (b) 1927
   (c) 1942
   (d) 1949

11. since
    (a) 1903
    (b) 1913
    (c) 1930
    (d) 1933

9. _____ it achieved
   self government.
   (a) the same year
   (b) seven years after
   (c) seventeen years after
   (d) twenty-seven years after

12. for more than
    (a) 2 centuries
    (b) 10 centuries
    (c) 12 centuries
    (d) 20 centuries

10. (a) the clergy
    (b) the teachers
    (c) the landlords
    (d) the politicians

Check your answers. Then continue working in your book. This is the end of the taped section of Lecture 6.

STOP THE TAPE.

C. Post-listening Activity

TRUE–FALSE STATEMENTS

In this exercise, you are given eleven statements about the lecture on Ireland and its first and second languages. Read each statement carefully, check your notes, and then come to a decision as to whether the statement is true or false according to the information presented by the lecturer. If the statement is true, place a T in the blank space next to the number of the statement. If it is false or inaccurate, place an F in the blank. Remember to refer to your notes before coming to your decision.

1. ____ Northern Ireland and the Republic of Ireland occupy the same island, but they are two separate nations today.

2. ____ Learning and culture flourished in Ireland between 400 and 500 A.D.

3. ____ When England gained control of Ireland, the Irish fought at first, but then accepted English rule peacefully.

4. ____ Throughout the eighteenth century, the Irish suffered from economic exploitation, but they did have religious and political freedom.

5. ____ The failure of the potato crop brought starvation to the people who left Ireland in the eighteenth century.

6. ____ The English language began to replace the Irish language because Englishmen, not Irishmen, held power in government, in the church, and on the economic front.

7. ____ The people of the southern part of the island of Ireland elected to separate politically from England.

8. ____ Before the mid-1940s, knowledge of the national language was not a requirement for teacher certification in Ireland.

9. ____ Today the Irish government still prints all of its documents in English only.

10. ____ The Irish people must understand the English language in order to read newspaper articles in their country today.

CHECK YOUR ANSWERS.

11. ____ The Irish language has been spoken in Ireland for just a thousand years.

D. Follow-up Activities

TOPICS FOR DISCUSSION OR WRITING

---

1. Are there any foreign languages used in your country? What are they? For what purpose and by whom are these languages used? Are they, for example, used for trade, education, international relations, and so on?

2. State several reasons why you are studying English as a second language.

3. Give several examples of foreign words that are commonly used in your native language. State the languages the words have been borrowed from. Group the foreign words into categories, such as business, food, clothing, science, and so on.

Women's Liberation:
The Search for Equality

A. Pre-listening Activities

PREVIEW OF CONTENT

The Women's Liberation Movement has become one of the most talked-about, and one of the most important, social movements of the twentieth century in the United States, and in many other countries throughout the entire world. It has, for better or for worse, altered the course of American politics, education, employment, and it has even changed the family structure. It has had, as a result, a tremendous impact on the lives of millions of American men, women, and children. In this lecture we will be dealing mainly with some of the background of the Movement and with the impact the Women's Liberation Movement has had on the political, economic, and social system of the United

States, but this does not mean that its influence has not been felt in other countries. It certainly has been, and in all probability it will be, felt in even more countries in the future.

The speaker starts the lecture by pointing out the major topics that will be touched upon during the presentation. She mentions that she will be talking about American women's struggle to gain equal rights and treatment in the fields of (1) politics, (2) education, (3) employment, and (4) the home. Listen carefully for the changes in topic as the lecture unfolds. During the presentation, the lecturer highlights some of the advances that women have made in the areas of (1) education and (2) politics, but she also notes that women still have a long way to go before they achieve true equality in the area of employment, as far as salary and job positions are concerned. The speaker gives quite a few examples, illustrations, and statistics to back up the points she makes during her talk.

PREVIEW OF VOCABULARY

Fill in each blank with one of the words listed below.

drafted	dependable	role	capable

1. A person's _____ is the characteristic social behavior expected of him or her.

2. A person you can depend on is one who is trustworthy and reliable. He or she is a _____ person.

3. If you are _____ , you are called into military service by your government. Men are usually _____ during wartime.

4. Many people have the ability or the power to do a job well. They are _____ workers.

plumber	disparity	second-class citizen

5. A worker who installs and repairs water and gas pipes is known as a _____ .

6. There is a _____ between the rich and poor in terms of purchasing power. This inequality causes great anger among poor people.

7. One who does not enjoy equal rights and treatment with the majority is a _____ in our society.

hiring	salary

8. A worker receives a fixed amount of money which is paid at regular times, such as once a week, for the work done. The worker receives a _____ for the work he or she does.

9. _____ a worker is the act of agreeing to pay money in return for work done.

CHECK YOUR ANSWERS.

PREVIEW OF SENTENCES

These are some of the sentences that you will hear in the lecture.

1. This seems to indicate that greater numbers of today's women are successfully managing to combine careers outside the home with the traditional *roles* of wife, mother, and homemaker.

2. Many women took the jobs of the men who were *drafted* into military service during World War II.

3. Women proved themselves to be *capable, dependable* workers.

4. Women workers do not yet receive equal treatment in the job market, either in the area of *hiring,* or in the area of *salary.*

5. Perhaps one of the reasons for the *disparity* in pay between men and women is that most women in the United States work in low-paying jobs.

6. Women are now working as corporate executives, officers in the armed forces, politicians, lawyers, and even as construction workers, *plumbers,* policewomen, and astronauts.

7. Women are no longer willing to accept the idea of being *second-class citizens* in their homes, in their marriages, at work, or in school.

B. Listening Activities

NOTE-TAKING MODEL

START THE TAPE.

You are about to hear a lecture about Women's Liberation, or what is often referred to as Women's Lib. As you listen to the lecture, you should be looking at the Note-Taking Model. After you have listened to the lecture once while following the model, you will listen to it again, at which time you will have the opportunity to take your own notes on the information contained in the lecture.

Women's Liberation: The Search for Equality

Women's Lib. Mov. — impt. soc. mov. (world + U.S.)
'60 & '70s   — eq. rights: pol. ed. empl. home

pol.   — powerful force:
                 U.S.   — 70 m. wom. vot. — voting age = 18 U.S.
                         +7 m.   "   "   than men

ed.   — better ed.
                 '50   — 7% wom. 18–24 in coll.
                 '80   — 30% "   "   "   "
                 today U.S.   — 5 m. wom. coll. grad.
                              (2.3 m. fewer than men; # wom. grad.
                              grow)

empl.   — "   " — 42% workers   — wom. (38.8 m.)
                 1900   — 20%
                 today   — careers + wife, mother + homemaker
? inc.?   years ago — work till marr. or child.

W.W. II — enter job market — men draft.
indep. + cap. workers
Japan. manager; women → prod. ↑ 10%
→ labor cost ↓ 15%

after war — stayed — jobs

today—probs. — still not eq. — hiring & $
'78 coll. ed. man — $15,446 (56% higher)
" " " woman — $8,633

reason for low pay — 33 1/3% wom. — bookkeep. sec. cl. = low pay
16% " — profess. tech. doc. teach. sci.
— have babies — lose senior.
corp. exec. officers pol. law.
const. plumb. police + astro.

20th C. — no 2nd class citizen
— better ed. inc. job opp.
— husb. help (house & child)
— new opp. free., + resp.

NOTE-TAKING EXERCISE

Are you ready to listen to the lecture again and to take your own notes on it? There will be less repetition of information in this exercise than there previously was, so you must begin to catch the information the first time you hear it. Check the *Word Guide* before the lecture starts. O.K., let's begin.

Word Guide

Women's Liberation Movement / bookkeepers / secretaries / clerks / doctors / teachers / scientists/ corporate executives / officers in the armed forces / politicians / lawyers / construction workers / plumbers / policewomen / astronauts / second-class citizens

_____

_____

_____

_____

_____

_____

_____

_____

_____

_____

_____

_____

_____

MULTIPLE-CHOICE QUESTIONS

You will now hear eleven questions about the lecture on Women's Lib. You will hear each question spoken two times, but the questions will, as usual, not be written out for you. You must read the four possible answer choices after hearing a question. You will then check your notes to find the correct answer to the question you heard. When you have found the correct answer, you must mark your choice by putting an X next to the letter (a), (b), (c), or (d)—whichever is the best answer.

For example:

You will hear: "When did women first begin to gain equal rights and treatment in the U.S.?"

You will read in your book:

> in the
> (a) 1930s and '40s
> (b) 1940s and '50s
> (c) 1950s and '60s
> X (d) 1960s and '70s

In checking your notes, you should have found that "it was in the 1960s and '70s in the United States that women really began to gain equal rights and treatment." You might have thought that choice (c) was partly correct in that the 1960s were mentioned in the answer; however, the more correct answer to the question was letter (d), the 1960s and '70s; therefore, letter (d) was the best choice. Be sure that you choose the *best answer* to each question.

1. (a) 7 million
   (b) 17 million
   (c) 63 million
   (d) 70 million

2. (a) 07%
   (b) 17%
   (c) 20%
   (d) none of the above

3. (a) 07%
   (b) 13%
   (c) 20%
   (d) 23%

4. more than
   (a) 2.3 million
   (b) 5.0 million
   (c) 7.3 million
   (d) none of the above

5. (a) 2.3 million
   (b) 5.0 million
   (c) 7.3 million
   (d) none of the above

6. (a) 07%
   (b) 20%
   (c) 40%
   (d) 50%

7. (a) productivity rose, and labor cost did, too.
   (b) productivity rose, but labor cost declined.
   (c) productivity declined, and labor cost did, too.
   (d) productivity declined, but labor cost increased.

8. (a) $6,833.00
   (b) $8,633.00
   (c) $15,446.00
   (d) none of the above

9. (a) $6,833.00
   (b) $8,633.00
   (c) $15,446.00
   (d) none of the above

10. (a) 16%
    (b) 33 1/3%
    (c) 66 2/3%
    (d) none of the above

11. (a) 06%
    (b) 16%
    (c) 33 1/3%
    (d) 50%

Check your answers. Then continue working in your book. This is the end of the taped section of Lecture 7.

STOP THE TAPE.

C. Post-listening Activity

TRUE-FALSE STATEMENTS

Read the following statements about the information contained in the lecture on Women's Liberation. Decide whether each statement is correct or incorrect based on the information you were given by the speaker. If the statement is correct, place a T in the blank space next to the number of the statement. If it is incorrect, place an F in the blank space. Change those statements that are incorrect into correct statements. Use your notes.

1. ____ There are a good deal fewer male than female voters in the U.S. today.

2. ____ During the first half of this decade, less than 10 percent of the women in the eighteen- to twenty-four age category were college students.

3. ____ Today 2.3 million more men than women have obtained college educations in the U.S.

4. ____ Sixty-four percent of the work force in the U.S. is made up of men.

5. ____ In the past most women customarily worked outside the home, even after they had children.

6. ____ The influx of women into the labor force is attributed to the onset of the First World War.

7. _____ The Japanese factory manager implied that women workers are more efficient workers than the male assembly line workers.

8. _____ A woman earns on the average $.90 for every dollar a man makes.

9. _____ Women traditionally have taken the lower-paying jobs in the job market.

10. _____ Loss of seniority is one of the reasons why, on the average, women earn less money than men do.

CHECK YOUR ANSWERS.

11. _____ The lecturer implies that modern-day American women are much happier than their grandmothers were.

D. Follow-up Activities

TOPICS FOR DISCUSSION OR WRITING

1. Discuss the roles women in your country play in (a) politics; (b) education; (c) the job market; and (d) the home.

2. Should women who have children work outside the home? Explain why or why not.

3. Are their fields of employment that are particularly suitable for women? What are they? Are there certain fields that are particularly unsuitable for women? What are they? Touch upon such fields as teaching, police work, the armed forces, construction work, and medicine in your discussion. Include any additional fields of employment that you can think of in your answer.

4. Should men help with the housework and the raising of children? Explain why they should or why they should not.

The Panama Canal:
A Great Engineering Achievement

A. Pre-listening Activities

PREVIEW OF CONTENT

The Panama Canal is located in the Central American country of Panama. It connects the Atlantic with the Pacific Ocean. Although it was constructed in the early 1900s, it is still a busy waterway through which thousands of ships pass each year. When it was first built, it was considered a wonder of technology.

The lecturer starts off with a description of the location and size of the Canal. She then gives an example of the way in which the Canal stimulated East-West trade by shortening the travel time between the East and West Coasts of the United States. There are a lot of facts in this section of the lecture that need to be gotten down. Next she turns to giving a brief history of the early, and unsuccessful Spanish attempt to construct a Canal in the Panama region in the sixteenth century. She then brings the talk around to the French and then the American attempts to build the Canal. Here again she cites quite a few dates, names, and figures to back up what she says. She also discusses the difficulties faced by the engineers and workers in the actual construction of the Canal. At this point, she changes topic and starts to describe the actual working of the Canal. She describes the dimensions of the Canal's locks and makes note of the inadequacy of the Canal in terms of the locks' small size. The lecture ends with brief mention of the dispute that arose between Panama and the United States concerning control of the Canal and the Canal Zone.

PREVIEW OF VOCABULARY

Fill in each blank with one of the words listed below. Use your dictionary to check the meaning of an item you are not familiar with.

survey   toll   fame

1. Money that is paid for the privilege of using a highway, bridge, or a canal is a _____ .

2. The Panama Canal is not famous because it is so large; the _____ of the Panama Canal is not in its size, but in its engineering excellence.

3. The king ordered his engineers to make a careful examination of the Panama area to learn whether or not a canal could be built there. He ordered a _____ of the area.

concession   to abandon the undertaking   lock

4. An enclosed area in a canal which has gates at each end and which is used to raise and lower ships from one level to another is a _____ .

5. To stop working on a project is _____ .

6. When a government or controlling authority grants a privilege or right to a company, it grants a _____ .

| dispute | Inca Empire | strategic |

---

7. The South American civilization established in Peru in the 1400s before the Spanish Conquest began is known as the _____ .

8. A _____ involves a disagreement, quarrel, or fight.

9. That which is especially important to the national defense or economy of a country is _____ for that country.

CHECK YOUR ANSWERS.

PREVIEW OF SENTENCES

These are some of the sentences that you will hear in the lecture.

1. Let me say that the *fame* of the Panama Canal is not in its size.

2. The early Spaniards needed a more efficient way to ship the treasures of the *Inca Empire* and their other South American colonies back to Spain.

3. King Charles I of Spain ordered a *survey* of the Panama area to determine whether or not it was possible to construct a canal in the area.

4. Disease and what some have called mismanagement forced the French company *to abandon the undertaking.*

5. In June of 1902, the United States bought the French company's *concession.*

6. I might add that this certainly was a very profitable investment for the United States because recent figures show that the Panama Canal Company collected $134 million in *tolls* on the Canal in one year alone.

7. As for the actual working of the Panama Canal, it has three sets of water-filled chambers or what are more commonly called *locks*.

8. Before I finish up, I'll say a word or two about the *dispute* that arose in the 1960s concerning the control of both the Canal and the Canal Zone.

9. The treaty provided for Panama to gain full control of the *strategic* waterway by the year 2000.

B. Listening Activities

NOTE-TAKING MODEL

START THE TAPE.

Now as you listen to the lecture about the Panama Canal, you should be looking at the Note-Taking Model. After you have listened to the lecture once while following the model, you will have a chance to listen to it another time. You will then have to take your own notes on the information contained in the lecture.

The Panama Canal: A Great Engineering Achievement

location	— conn. A & P oceans
	— at narrowest part — Panama
size	— fame — not size (50.72 mi. — 81.65 k. long)
	Suez 103 ” — 166 ” ”
importance	— eng. achievement
	— changed trade rts. = Orient & West closer
	A & P coast — U.S. closer
	— before: N.Y. to S.F. — 13,000 mi. — 20,930 k.
	— after: ” ” ” = 5,200 ” — 8,370 ”
	— east coast S. Am. ⎫
	—Pac. ” Asia ⎭ closer
hist.	— early Sp. (unsucc.) — ship treasures (Inca Emp. &
	S. A. col. — Au. & Ag. → Spain)
	— 1534 — Charles I — survey — area — impossible
	— no mach, tech.
	— 1882 — Fr. co. (de Lesseps — Suez) — disease & ⎫ abandon
	mismanag. ⎭

                        — 1902   — U.S. bought Fr. concession — $10 mil. to Panama
                        — 1903   — treaty U.S. build, oper. & gov. C. Zone   —
                        (5 mi. — 8 k.) either side
                        — 1000's worked (Gorgas & Goethals)
                        — 5,609 died dis. & acc.
                        — cost $380 mil.
                        — coll. $134 m— 1 yr. tolls

phys. descript.   — 3 sets   — locks   — raise & lower ships
                                              — pairs   — both — same time
                        — trip   — 7—8 hrs.
                        — ea. lock   — 1,000' (300 m.) l.
                                        110' (33 m.) w.
                                         70' (21 m.) d.
                        — by 2000, larger locks needed
dispute   — '60   — control of P.C. & C.Z.
late '70 treaty   — Panama control   — 2000

NOTE-TAKING EXERCISE

All right, why don't you now listen to the lecture again. Only this time, take your own notes on the information you hear. There will be less repetition of information, so try to get down the facts the first time you hear them. Check the *Word Guide* before the lecture begins.

Word Guide

the Atlantic Ocean / the Pacific Ocean / North and South America / King Charles I of Spain / the Inca Empire / the Suez Canal / Ferdinand de Lesseps / Dr. William Gorgas / Colonel George Goethals

_____

_____

_____

_____

_____

_____

_____

_____

_____

_____

_____

_____

_____

_____

MULTIPLE-CHOICE QUESTIONS

Now you will be able to check whether you: (1) understood the lecture; (2) understand questions about the lecture content; and (3) took sufficient notes to find the answers to the questions you will hear. All right, let's begin this exercise. You will hear twelve questions about the information you heard in the lecture. You are to select from the choices—(a), (b), (c), or (d)—the phrase or statement that correctly answers the question you hear. You should, naturally, refer to your notes when making the choices, so keep your notes handy. Are you ready?

1. (a) 50.72 miles
   (b) 70.52 miles
   (c) 63.81 kilometers
   (d) 83.61 kilometers

2. (a) 2,930
   (b) 13,000
   (c) 20,000
   (d) 20,930

3. it shortened the trip by
   (a) 3,000
   (b) 7,800
   (c) 8,700
   (d) 13,000

4. to transport the treasures of the
   (a) Inca Empire to Spain
   (b) Spanish Empire to England
   (c) Panamanian Empire to Spain
   (d) Inca Empire to its other South American colonies

5. (a) 340
   (b) 344
   (c) 348
   (d) 352

6. because of
   (a) money problems
   (b) the lack of workers
   (c) engineering difficulties
   (d) disease and mismanagement

7. (a) $1,000,000
   (b) $10,000,000
   (c) $11,000,000
   (d) $100,000,000

8. (a) $18,000,000
   (b) $30,000,000
   (c) $308,000,000
   (d) $380,000,000

9. (a) $10,000,000
   (b) $134,000,000
   (c) $246,000,000
   (d) $380,000,000

10. (a) 300 feet
    (b) 300 meters
    (c) 1,000 meters
    (d) none of the above

11. (a) 110 feet
    (b) 340 meters
    (c) 110 meters
    (d) none of the above

12. (a) 21 meters
    (b) 33 meters
    (c) 300 meters
    (d) none of the above

Check your answers. Then continue working in your book. This is the end of the taped section of Lecture 8.

STOP THE TAPE.

C. Post-listening Activity

TRUE–FALSE STATEMENTS

Read the following statements. Determine, with the help of your notes, whether the statements are true or false. Some of the statements require that you make inferences about the information you were given during the lecture.

1. ____ The Panama Canal cuts through the Central American country of Panama.

2. ____ The Suez Canal is not as long as the Panama Canal.

3. ____ Because of the Panama Canal, ships traveling from Europe to Japan did not have to travel around the tip of South America.

4. ____ There had been a good deal of interest in building a canal in the Panama region three centuries before one was ever constructed there.

5. ____ Reports to King Charles I of Spain indicated optimism about the possibility of constructing a canal in the Panama area.

6. ____ The early Spaniards attempted to build a sea-level canal to connect the Atlantic with the Pacific Ocean.

7. ____ Advances in engineering made it possible to attempt the construction of a canal in the Panama area in the early twentieth century.

8. ____ The engineer who built the Suez Canal directed the construction of the unsuccessful attempt by a French company to build a canal in the Panama region.

9. ____ Hospital records indicate that construction of the Canal went smoothly.

10. ____ The United States did not realize a profit from building the Canal.

11. ____ Each Canal lock is longer than it is wide.

12. ____ Each lock is about seventy meters deep.

13. ____ By the year 2000, no ships will be traveling through the Panama Canal because the locks are so small.

14. ____ Panama is in full control of the Panama Canal at this time.

CHECK YOUR ANSWERS.

D. Follow-up Activities

TOPICS FOR DISCUSSION OR WRITING

1. When the Panama Canal opened, it changed the trade routes of the world and dramatically increased international trade. What other technological developments have had a great impact on international travel, communication, and trade?

2. Why are both the Panama and the Suez Canal considered *strategic* waterways? For which countries and for what reasons are they strategic?

3. Compare the dimensions of the Panama Canal (including the dimensions of the locks) with those of the Suez Canal. (You can find this information in an encyclopedia or an almanac.)

4. Write brief profiles of Ferdinand de Lesseps, George Goethals, and William Gorgas. (You will find information about these men in an encyclopedia.)

5. Research and write about another important canal that is a major commercial waterway.

T. E. Lawrence:
Lawrence of Arabia

A. Pre-listening Activities

PREVIEW OF CONTENT

The lecture you are going to hear is narrative in form. It is the story of T. E. Lawrence's life told against the background of the start and finish of World War I. The speaker starts off with a word or two about Lawrence's background—about where and when he was born; where he went to school; and what courses of study he pursued in college. He then leaves off talking about Lawrence and begins to talk briefly about the political situation in the Middle East at the outbreak of World War I. He here explains why Lawrence was sent to help with the Arab revolt (to help incite Arab rebellion against the Turkish Empire). He goes on to draw a picture of Lawrence and his Arab comrades fighting a guerilla war to defeat the Turkish forces. Here the lecturer jumps to the end of the war and discusses Lawrence's inability to promote Arab independence from France and Great Britain. He describes Lawrence as a man who feels that he has betrayed his former comrades. The last section of the lecture covers the period in Lawrence's life from his leaving the Colonial Office in 1922 until his death in mid-1930. He says that the war hero withdrew from the public and avoided all fame and glory he might have received because of his excellent fighting record. The lecturer draws his narrative to an end with some words about the controversy that surrounds this Englishman. Some people, he says, consider Lawrence a saint. Others believe he was a devil. The lecturer points out that, above all, he was a colorful, complex personality.

LECTURE OUTLINE—A TOPIC OUTLINE

I. Life before World War I
    A. Childhood
    B. College days

II. Life during World War I
    A. Assignment to British Intelligence
    B. Guerilla warfare against the Turks
    C. Victory for the Arabs and Allies.

III. Life after World War I
    A. Attending the Paris Peace Conference
    B. Quitting the Colonial Office
    C. Enlisting in the Royal Air Force and Tank Corps.

IV. Death and Controversy

PREVIEW OF VOCABULARY

Fill in the blank with one of the appropriate items.

pseudonym	Hejaz	archaeology	guerilla-type tactics

1. _____ are procedures of warfare carried on by members of a small, independent band of fighters who attack the enemy in sudden, surprising raids.

2. _____ is the western section of Saudi Arabia.

3. The study of an ancient civilization and culture by digging up and studying its remains is _____ .

4. A name adopted by a person who wishes to hide his or her real identity or name is referred to as a _____ .

---

a living legend   intelligence section   to weld   scattered

---

5. The _____ of the army is the branch of the army that collects and studies information that will help the army to attack the enemy or to protect itself.

6. The term _____ is applied to a person whose extraordinary actions bring him or her publicity, fame and admiration while he or she is still alive.

7. To join closely is _____ .

8. Saying that the Arab forces were disunited and separated is saying that the forces were _____ .

Ottoman Empire   Allies   tank corps

---

9. During World War I, the _____ were Great Britain, Russia, Belgium, Serbia, Japan, and Italy.

10. The section of the army that uses armored, slow-moving vehicles that are armed with powerful guns and that can attack an enemy over very rough ground is the _____ .

11. The Turkish empire founded in 1300 A.D. and replaced in 1922 by the Republic of Turkey is designated the _____ . At the height of its power, it included Turkey, the Barbary states, Egypt, Arabia, and the Balkan Peninsula.

---

seclusion   anonymity   ironic

---

12. The state of being alone or living apart from people is called _____ .

13. The state of being unknown by name is _____ .

14. Irony is a condition that is opposite to what would usually be expected. It is _____ that so many rich people are so unhappy.

CHECK YOUR ANSWERS.

PREVIEW OF SENTENCES

Here are some of the sentences taken from the lecture.

1. While he was at Oxford, Lawrence became keenly interested in *archaeology.*

2. T. E. Lawrence was attached to the *intelligence section* of the British army at the outbreak of World War I.

3. Lawrence helped to organize the Arab revolt against the *Ottoman Empire.*

4. Lawrence *welded* the *scattered* Arab forces into a fighting unit.

5. By using *guerilla-type tactics* instead of conventional warfare, he and a few thousand Arabs succeeded in tying down the Turkish forces.

6. Under his leadership, the guerillas sabotaged the supply trains in *Hejaz.*

7. The defeat of the Turkish forces led to victory for both the Arabs and the *Allies.*

8. After the war, Lawrence enlisted in the Royal Air Force, and later in the *tank corps.*

9. He enlisted in the Air Force and the tank corps under *pseudonyms.*

10. Lawrence sought *seclusion* and *anonymity* after the war.

11. It seems *ironic,* indeed, that after all the dangers Lawrence had faced, and all the battles he had fought during the war, he was killed in a motorcycle accident.

12. Lawrence was an unusual, strange, and complex Englishman, a *living legend* of the early 1900s.

B. Listening Activities

NOTE-TAKING MODEL

START THE TAPE.

   I'm now going to talk about the colorful Lawrence of Arabia. As you listen to the lecture about his life before, during, and after World War I, look at the Note-Taking Model. There are quite a few abbreviations and symbols in the model. It may seem a bit confusing at first, but you should try to follow along as the lecture is presented. You may choose to use different symbols or to abbreviate words differently, but you should notice that all the important information and all the facts have been taken down in the notes. All right, let's begin this lecture on T. E. Lawrence—Lawrence of Arabia, as he is sometimes called.

T. E. Lawrence: Lawrence of Arabia

T.E.L.   — born 8/15/88   — Wales
            child   — France
            youth   — Oxford, Eng.
            college   — archaeo. (M.E.)
                             Arabic
            — W.W. I (1914) — intell. sec. Br. army — war — Germ & Turk.
                             Br. wanted Ar. reb. → vict. Eng.
                             O. Emp.   — cont. whole A. Pen.
            however   — Ahab; Fetah   — prep. reb. (Feisal al Hussein)

Lawrence   — sent to Arabia → fall — O.E.
   "   — org. rev. — '16 — '18 (Feisal I)

Ar. lifestyle: lang., cloth., camel
Ar. lib. & indep.
guerr./conv. tactics sabot. supp. tr.   — Hejaz
                                       vict. Allies &
                                       def. Turks
— end. W.W. I — Br. del.   — Paris Peace Conf. '19   — (Jan '19)
                         — unsucc. → Ar. lib. & keep prom.
                           '21 — '22 adviser   —M.E. Div. Col. Off.
                                 disapp. — Br. pol. → resigned ”   ”
                           ”   ” 8/30/22   — R.A.F.; tank — 323
                           (pseudo.) — sec. & anon.
                           books — *7 Pillars of Wis.* (A. exper.)
                  life end   — country road   — 5/35 — motorcycle acc.

— hero, traitor — saint — devil
   admir.   — cour. dedic. leader
   critics   — ambit. wk. confus.
   unusual, st. complex   —   liv. legend 1900s

NOTE-TAKING EXERCISE

This time you are to take notes on the lecture about Lawrence of Arabia as you listen to it. Make sure that you have checked the *Word Guide* before we begin the exercise. You will listen to the entire lecture without interruption. This will test your ability to listen and take notes on a great deal of information.

Word Guide

Thomas Edward Lawrence / Wales / Oxford / Germany / Turkey / the Ottoman Empire / the Arabian Peninsula / the Ahab / the Fetah / Feisal al Hussein / the Paris Peace Conference / the Colonial Office / the Royal Air Force / *The Seven Pillars of Wisdom*

_____

_____

_____

_____

_____

_____

_____

_____

_____

_____

_____

_____

_____

MULTIPLE-CHOICE QUESTIONS

In the following exercise, you will hear ten questions. You are to select from the choices (a), (b), (c), or (d) the phrase or statement that *correctly* answers the questions. You should refer to your notes when making your choice.

1. in the
   (a) summer of 1888
   (b) fall of 1888
   (c) winter of 1888
   (d) spring of 1888

2. from
   (a) 1916 to 1917
   (b) 1916 to 1918
   (c) 1916 to 1920
   (d) none of the above

3. (a) Turkish forces
   (b) Turkish communications
   (c) the supply trains
   (d) all of the above

4. (a) the Arab
   (b) the British
   (c) the Turkish
   (d) none of the above

5. in the
   (a) division of the Royal Air Force
   (b) intelligence section of the British army
   (c) Middle East Division of the Colonial Office
   (d) British delegation to the Paris Peace Conference

6. (a) He returned to Arabia.
   (b) He became an archaeologist.
   (c) He sought fame and glory.
   (d) He enlisted in the Royal Air Force.

7. in
   (a) August, 1888
   (b) August, 1922
   (c) March, 1923
   (d) May, 1935

8. (a) the Paris Peace Conference
   (b) T. E. Lawrence's Arabian exploits
   (c) a soldier's life in the Turkish army
   (d) the rise and fall of the Ottoman Empire

9. He was almost
   (a) 45 years old
   (b) 47 years old
   (c) 49 years old
   (d) 51 years old

10. as a
    (a) hero and a saint
    (b) confused and weak man
    (c) courageous leader of men
    (d) all of the above

Check your answers. Then continue working in your book. This is the end of the taped section of Lecture 9.

STOP THE TAPE.

C. Post-listening Activity

TRUE–FALSE STATEMENTS

T = The statement is accurate according to the information presented in the lecture.

F = The statement is inaccurate according to the information presented in the lecture.

? = The accuracy or inaccuracy of the statement cannot be determined from the information presented in the lecture.

1. ____ Lawrence led a very happy childhood.

2. ____ Lawrence first studied Arabic while he was in Arabia.

3. ____ Lawrence lived in at least three countries during his youth.

4. ____ British leaders wanted an Arab rebellion against the Turks to break out mainly for the benefit of England.

5. ____ Lawrence was probably sent to Arabia because he could speak Arabic.

6. ____ Feisal al Hussein visited England after the war.

7. ____ Lawrence and his Arab comrades were effective guerilla warriors.

8. ____ Lawrence was able to secure the formation of independent Arab nations after the war.

9. ____ The Paris Peace Conference was held five years after the start of the war.

10. ____ The supply trains in Hejaz were Turkish supply trains.

11. ____ Lawrence worked with some of his old college friends in the Colonial Office.

12. ____ Lawrence left the Colonial Office a happy man.

13. ____ After the war Lawrence sought fame and glory by enlisting in the RAF.

14. ____ Lawrence's motorcycle crashed into an oncoming car.

15.____ People differ in their opinions of Lawrence.

16.____ "Lawrence of Arabia" is the pseudonym of Thomas Edward Lawrence.

17.____ Lawrence is a living legend of our time.

CHECK YOUR ANSWERS.

D. Follow-up Activities

TOPICS FOR DISCUSSION OR WRITING

1. Both conventional and guerilla-type tactics have been used in fighting wars. Give an example of the use of each type of warfare by countries at war.

2. Was T. E. Lawrence a hero or a traitor? Did Lawrence help or hinder the cause of Arab liberation and independence? Explain your position.

3. When did your country secure its independence? How was this achieved?

4. Write a short profile of a controversial military leader.

The Dust Bowl:
Nature Against Mankind

A. Pre-listening Activities

PREVIEW OF CONTENT

From 1929 to approximately 1934, the United States experienced a major economic disaster—the Depression. The Stock Market Crash of 1929 marked the end of post-World War I prosperity for the United States. In 1929 prices of American stocks fell sharply. It is estimated that stock losses for the 1929–1931 period alone totaled $50 billion.

The country's economic situation was made worse by the natural disaster that struck the Great Plains states of Colorado, Kansas, New Mexico, South Dakota, Texas, and Oklahoma. Drought and dust storms destroyed many of the Great Plains farms and brought poverty, hunger, and death to these farmers. An account of this natural disaster is given in the lecture that follows.

The lecturer opens his talk with a description of the unusual and terrible weather that hit the United States in the 1930s. He mentions that the North and East of the country experienced floods and windstorms, while the western states experienced unusual heat and drought. This lack of rainfall and the onset of the dust storms brought suffering to people and devastation to the farmlands of the Great Plains states. He talks about the heavy dust storms, the "black blizzards," that destroyed so many small farms. Two specific examples of the black blizzards are given: the South Dakota blizzard and the Texas dust storm. He describes the resulting destruction these storms brought to the small farmers of the Great Plains section of the country. The lecturer here digresses briefly to give a possible explanation of what caused the "Dust Bowl"—the term that is used to describe the area of the western United States that suffered from severe lack of rain and from dust storms in the 1930s. The speaker says that the catastrophe—the disaster—was brought on primarily by poor farming practices: by farmers' allowing farm animals to eat all the grass and vegetation in the area; and by their planting crops so often that the land would not produce any more crops. He uses the terms "overgraze" and "overplow" to describe these two poor farming practices. The speaker says that this abuse of the land, together with the drought that hit the Great Plains area, caused such hardship for the Great Plains farmers, who were called "Okies," that they fled from the Dust Bowl area to California where they thought they would find work and happiness. He says that for these poor farmers California was their only hope, their salvation. For some it was. For so many, California was not!

The talk ends with the lecturer pointing out that the Depression years were awful for many western farmers and also for eastern city people.

LECTURE OUTLINE—A TOPIC OUTLINE

I. The Weather versus Mankind
   A. Floods and windstorms
   B. Cold and heat

II. Ecological Catastrophe for the Great Plains
   A. Unusual amount of rainfall
   B. Destruction of farmland
      1. Overgrazing and overplowing
      2. Drought

III. Drought in the Great Plains in the 1930s
   A. First black blizzard—South Dakota
   B. Second black blizzard—Texas
   C. Oklahoma black blizzard

IV. Destruction of Farms
   A. Migration from Dust Bowl to California
   B. Steinbeck—*Grapes of Wrath*

V. Hardship for All Americans

PREVIEW OF VOCABULARY

Fill in the blanks with the appropriate vocabulary items.

---

drought	Great Plains	Depression years	Dust Bowl

---

1. The years (especially the years during the 1930s) during which there was a drastic reduction of economic activity in the United States are known as the _____ .

2. The _____ are the high, extensive grasslands of the western United States. The area is generally flat, treeless, and semi-dry. The region contains the eastern part of North and South Dakota, Nebraska, Kansas, and Oklahoma; the eastern parts of Montana, Wyoming, Colorado, and New Mexico; and the north-western part of Texas.

3. A long period of dry weather with continued lack of rain is designated a _____ .

4. The _____ is the area of the western United States that suffered from severe drought and dust storms (especially during the 1930s).

---

arable land   ecological catastrophe   meager

---

5. _____ is synonymous with the terms "small" and "slight."

6. An _____ occurs when the balance between the harmonious relationship among plants, animals, humans, and nature is upset or disturbed because of some natural or artificial change.

7. _____ is land that is suitable for plowing and for growing crops.

Okies   overgraze   overplow   drudgery

---

8. To turn the soil and plant crops so often that the land will no longer yield crops is to _____ .

9. To _____ is to allow farm animals, especially cattle, to eat all the grass or vegetation in one area.

10. Work that is hard, without interest, and disagreeable is _____ .

11. Oklahoma tenant farmers who were forced to leave their dust- and drought-stricken farms, and who went west as migration workers in the 1930s in the United States, were called _____ .

CHECK YOUR ANSWERS.

PREVIEW OF SENTENCES

These are some of the sentences that you will hear in the lecture.

1. One of the more tragic aspects of the *Depression years* of the 1930s was the weather.

2. One of the worst problems of the time was the combination of heat, *drought,* and the strong, hot, dusty winds which were known as black blizzards.

3. For years conservationists had warned that an *ecological catastrophe* was coming over the *Great Plains* of the United States.

4. Because of the *meager* amount of yearly rainfall, 100 counties in the states of Colorado, Kansas, New Mexico, Texas, and Oklahoma had been called the *Dust Bowl* even in the 1920s.

5. Farmers allowed their cattle to *overgraze* the land, and they themselves *overplowed* the land.

6. In 1934 government conservationists estimated that thirty-five million acres of *arable land* had been completely destroyed because of overplowing.

7. Among the most unfortunate of all the migrants who were forced to abandon their farms were the Oklahoma farmers. They were called *Okies.*

8. What the migrants actually found when they reached their "Promised Land" was just more *drudgery,* more hardship, and incredible poverty.

B. Listening Activities

NOTE-TAKING MODEL

START THE TAPE.

As you listen to the lecture about the Dust Bowl, look at the Note-Taking Model. Remember, your notes may not look exactly like the model, but you should attempt to use some of the techniques used in the model—noting down the factual data; using abbreviations and, if possible, symbols; writing neatly; and so on.

All right. Let's get started with the lecture.

The Dust Bowl: Nature Against Mankind

Dep.   — weather vs. mankind
                         floods, windstorms/no. & east — maj. E. rivers
                         flooded
                         Ohio R. flood '37   — destroyed ½ m. homes (3,678
                         lives lost — floods)

                         weather   — maj. prob. U.S.   — winters/cold
                                                        summers/hot — '36
                                                        Kansas — 60 days
                                                        100° F = 37° C
                         Comb. heat/drought/winds = black blizzards   —
                         7/24/36 — 120° F = 49° C

conserv. warned: ecolog. catastrophe for GP

generally   — GP rainfall = 20" = 51 cm   — 100 counties in
                         Colo. Kan. N.M. Tex. Okal. = Dust Bowl in '20s.

just before Dep. GP had extra heavy rain → new farms → overgraze & overplow
              cover veg. damaged & topsoil exposed
          35 m. acres — completely destroyed = 14,164,000 hectares
          100 m. "   — doomed — misuse   = 40,469,000 "

drought in GP   — Dust Bowl grew — 100 counties (5 states) '20s →
                         756 counties (19 states)   — 30s.

1st black blizz   — 11/33   — So. Dakota
                         sand = 30' high = 9 m.
                         dust cloud = 5 miles = 8 km
2nd "   "   — Texas   — farms → Saharas
another" "   — Okla.   — street lights on   — 3 weeks
                                     dust masks/temp. = 108° F = 42.2° C

Farmers ruined   — 60% pop. migrated from DB counties
                         1 Tex. county — from 40,000 → 1,000 people

                         Okies   — Steinbeck — *Grapes of Wrath* — '40
                         movie
                         Calif. = Promised Land but only more hardship

Americans suffered   — Dep. — natural & econ. disaster in U.S.

NOTE-TAKING EXERCISE

Now that you've heard the lecture once, you should be able to take some pretty good notes on the lecture information. Check the *Word Guide* before you begin.

Word Guide

the Ohio River / Kansas / degrees Fahrenheit / degrees Celsius / the Great Plains / Colorado / New Mexico / Texas / Oklahoma / Ireland / Sahara Desert / Okies / John Steinbeck / *The Grapes of Wrath* / California / the Promised Land

_____

_____

_____

_____

_____

_____

_____

_____

_____

_____

_____

_____

_____

_____

MULTIPLE-CHOICE QUESTIONS

In the following exercise, you will hear fourteen questions about the information you heard in the lecture. You are to select from the choices (a), (b), (c), or (d)—the phrase or statement that *correctly* answers the question you have heard. Always refer to your notes before making your choice.

1. (a) 3,678
   (b) 3,768
   (c) 3,876
   (d) none of the above

2. (a) 30.7°
   (b) 37.7°
   (c) 40.2°
   (d) 42.2°

3. on
   (a) June 4, 1930
   (b) June 24, 1930
   (c) July 4, 1936
   (d) July 24, 1936

4. (a) 14 million
   (b) 35 million
   (c) 40 million
   (d) 100 million

5. (a) 14,164,000
   (b) 30,469,000
   (c) 35,000,000
   (d) 40,469,000

6. million acres
   (a) 20
   (b) 35
   (c) 100
   (d) none of the above

7. (a) 5
   (b) 9
   (c) 14
   (d) 19

8. approximately
   (a) 50%
   (b) 70%
   (c) 100%
   (d) none of the above

9. kilometers
   (a) 8
   (b) 9
   (c) 30
   (d) none of the above

10. (a) 82°
    (b) 87°
    (c) 100°
    (d) 108°

11. (a) 20%
    (b) 40%
    (c) 60%
    (d) 80%

12. (a) 1,000
    (b) 30,000
    (c) 39,000
    (d) 40,000

13. (a) a book
    (b) a movie
    (c) both of the above
    (d) neither of the above

14. because
    (a) their farms were ruined
    (b) they hoped to find work there
    (c) they were looking for a better life there
    (d) all of the above

Check your answers. Then continue working in your book. This is the end of the taped section of Lecture 10.

STOP THE TAPE.

C. Post-listening Activity

TRUE-FALSE STATEMENTS

T = The statement is accurate according to the information presented in the lecture.

F = The statement is inaccurate according to the information presented in the lecture.

? = The accuracy or inaccuracy of the statement cannot be determined from the information presented in the lecture.

1.____ During the Depression years of the 1930s, it seemed as if the weather was working harmoniously with humanity.

2.____ The Ohio River Flood lasted for ten days.

3.____ The weather was a major problem in every section of the United States.

4.____ During the 1930s winters in the United States were unusually cold, and so were summers.

5.____ The black blizzards caused economic hardship for the Great Plains farmers.

6.____ Conservationists were happy that many new farms were being established in the Great Plains area.

7.____ The conservationists met with groups of small farmers.

8.____ The expected amount of rainfall equaled the received amount of rainfall in the Great Plains area just before the Depression years began.

9.____ Ireland experienced drought conditions in the nineteenth century.

10.____ The first black blizzard struck in November, 1933.

11.____ Street lights in Oklahoma had to be kept on day and night for twenty-one days straight.

12. ____ The term "Okie" was applied mainly to rich people.

CHECK YOUR ANSWERS.

13. ____ The natural disaster that hit the Great Plains also affected people in the eastern part of the country.

D. Follow-up Activities

TOPICS FOR DISCUSSION OR WRITING

1. Illustrate how the weather affects the kinds of crops grown in the region of your country that you come from.

2. Describe several poor farming practices. What can be done to correct such practices? Research this topic.

3. Discuss the interrelationship between bad weather and economic hardship for a country.

4. Describe a serious economic or natural disaster that your country has experienced. Include in the description an account of the nature of the disaster and its effects upon the economy of your country.

5. Earthquakes, floods, droughts, and typhoons are kinds of natural disasters. Discuss what attempts are made to predict and control such natural disasters.

John F. Kennedy:
Promise and Tragedy

John F. Kennedy

A. Pre-listening Activities

PREVIEW OF CONTENT

Millions of words have been written about the life and death of the young American president, John Fitzgerald Kennedy. Much of the writing has been emotional, with rather little regard for the actual facts. In the following lecture, you will hear an attempt at an objective assessment of President Kennedy's virtues and his faults; his strengths and his weaknesses; his idealism and his lack of realism. The lecturer organizes the talk around the following themes: Kennedy, the person; Kennedy, the international politician; Kennedy, the domestic politician; Kennedy, the social reformer. A topic outline of the organizational structure of the talk might take this form:

LECTURE OUTLINE—A TOPIC OUTLINE

I. Kennedy's Personal Life
   A. A place in legend
   B. A surprising person
   Did things earlier than most people
      1. Elected to Congress at 29
      2. Elected to the White House at 43
   C. Mishaps and tragedies
      1. Assassination at 46
      2. War injury and surgery
      3. Death of newborn son

II. Kennedy's Decision Making
   A. Question of how he made final decisions about:
      1. Invasion of the Bay of Pigs
      2. 1962 Russian attempt to install missiles in Cuba
      3. Deeper involvement of the U.S. in Vietnam
      4. 1963 atomic test ban treaty
   B. Idealism versus Realism
      1. Vision of a strong, interdependent NATO (North Atlantic Treaty Organization)
      2. The Alliance for Progress

III. Kennedy the International Diplomat versus Kennedy the Domestic Politician
   A. Effectiveness in the world of international diplomacy
   B. Successes in domestic programs—Congressional approval of:
      1. Creation of the Peace Corps
      2. Raising of the minimum wage
      3. Increase of social benefits
      4. Support for space flights
   C. Failures in domestic programs—Congressional disapproval of:
      1. Free medical care for people over 65
      2. Creation of a department of urban affairs for America's cities
      3. Federal aid to education
      4. Tax reform and tax reduction

IV. Responsibility for Legislation Benefiting Black Americans
   A. Bill to prohibit racial discrimination
   B. Bill to outlaw school segregation

V. Social Reform in U.S. Resulting from Assassination

PREVIEW OF VOCABULARY

Fill in the blanks with the appropriate item.

---

minimum wage   assassinated   mishap   discrimination

---

1. An unfortunate accident or a great misfortune is a
   _____ .

2. The _____ refers to the least amount of money
   per hour that an employer can pay for work done.

3. President Kennedy was _____ in 1963. He was
   murdered in Texas.

4. The unfair treatment of a person because of his or her particular
   race, religion, politics, or sex is termed _____ .

---

envision   chit-chat   social security benefits   segregation

---

5. The forced separation of black and white people is racial
   _____ .

6. To make small-talk or to have light or informal conversation with
   someone is to _____ .

7. To _____ something is to picture mentally some
   future event or happening.

8. _____ refer to the services and money the U.S.
   government provides to American citizens who are sixty-five
   years or older.

CHECK YOUR ANSWERS.

PREVIEW OF SENTENCES

Here are some of the sentences that you will encounter in the lecture.

1. At the age of forty-six, Kennedy was *assassinated.*

2. Kennedy suffered a series of *mishaps* and tragedies.

3. In his handling of American foreign policy, Kennedy *envisioned* a strong, interdependent Atlantic world.

4. To make small-talk—to *chit-chat*—with self-important American congressmen bored Kennedy.

5. Congress raised the *minimum wage.*

6. Congress also increased *social security benefits.*

7. Kennedy was responsible for the bill that prohibited *discrimination* in employment, and in public facilities.

8. Kennedy was responsible for the bill that outlawed school *segregation.*

B. Listening Activities

LECTURE OVERVIEW

START THE TAPE.

Before the lecturer begins her talk on J. F. Kennedy, let me give you a brief overview of the main ideas—the main topics—she's going to touch upon in her talk. This preview will help prepare you for the job of taking notes on a lecture the first time you listen to it. There is no Note-Taking Model given in this lecture presentation, so follow the Lecture Outline while you are listening to this Overview.

NOTE-TAKING EXERCISE

All right, now that you have some idea of the topics that are covered in the lecture and the vocabulary that is used, you should be able to take some pretty good notes on the material. It's not going to be easy because the lecture is long and has a lot of information, but this is the first time you have had to take notes on a lecture without hearing it once through while you were looking at a Note-Taking Model. Let's try it. Are you ready? Remember, check the *Word Guide* before you begin.

Word Guide

John Fitzgerald Kennedy / Congress / the White House / Robert Kennedy / the Bay of Pigs / Cuba / Vietnam / the North Atlantic Treaty Organization/ NATO / the Alliance for Progress / President Lyndon Johnson / the New Frontier

_____

_____

_____

_____

_____

_____

_____

_____

_____

_____

_____

_____

_____

_____

_____

_____

MULTIPLE-CHOICE QUESTIONS

In the following exercise, you will hear eleven questions on the Kennedy lecture. You are to select from the choices (a), (b), (c), or (d) the *correct answer* to the question you have heard. Be sure that you use your notes for reference.

1. (a) 20
   (b) 24
   (c) 30
   (d) 34

2. (a) 10
   (b) 14
   (c) 20
   (d) 29

3. (a) 40
   (b) 42
   (c) 44
   (d) 46

4. (a) 1951
   (b) 1953
   (c) both of the above
   (d) neither of the above

5. (a) 3
   (b) 5
   (c) 7
   (d) 9

6. (a) England
   (b) France
   (c) the United States
   (d) the Soviet Union

7. (a) the Peace Corps
   (b) the Alliance for Progress
   (c) increased social security benefits
   (d) the North Atlantic Treaty Organization

8. in
   (a) 1963
   (b) 1964
   (c) 1965
   (d) 1966

9. in
   (a) 1963
   (b) 1965
   (c) 1967
   (d) 1969

10. (a) establishment of the Peace Corps
    (b) the outlawing of school segregation
    (c) the raising of the minimum wage
    (d) the increasing of social security benefits

11. (a) Black Americans
    (b) Indian Americans
    (c) Mexican Americans
    (d) American women

STOP THE TAPE.

Check your answers. Then continue working in your book. This is the end of the taped section of Lecture 11.

C. Post-listening Activity

TRUE–FALSE STATEMENTS

T = The statement is accurate according to the information presented in the lecture.

F = The statement is inaccurate according to the information presented in the lecture.

? = The accuracy or inaccuracy of the statement cannot be determined from the information presented in the lecture.

1. ____ It is unusual for a man or woman younger than thirty to be elected to Congress.

2. ____ Kennedy's murder took place in the spring of 1963.

3. ____ Kennedy was assassinated by a lone assassin.

4. ____ Because Kennedy was young, well-educated, and rich, things went smoothly in his life.

5. ____ Kennedy's newborn son died in 1961.

6. ____ Kennedy's advisers took part in the entire process of his decision making.

7. ____ Kennedy had such an acute sense of history that he kept very careful records of what led up to his political decisions.

8. ____ There was friction among the members of the North Atlantic Treaty Organization (NATO) during Kennedy's presidency.

9. ____ Latin American countries benefited little from the Alliance for Progress.

10. ____ Kennedy was less effective in the role of domestic politician than in the role of international diplomat.

11. ____ The "New Frontier" refers to the western boundary of the United States during Kennedy's term in office.

12. ____ Increasing social security benefits provided extra money for America's "senior citizens."

13. ____ Under Kennedy the U.S. space exploration program expanded.

14. ____ Kennedy's plan to provide free medical care for people over sixty-five was rejected by the American Congress during his time in office.

CHECK YOUR ANSWERS.

15. ____ Kennedy is famous for the remark that Americans should not ask what they can do for their country, but what their country can do for them.

D. Follow-up Activities

TOPICS FOR DISCUSSION OR WRITING

1. Make a chronological outline of the important events in Kennedy's political life as listed in the lecture script. Begin the outline with 1947.

2. Illustrate how Kennedy's life was a mixture of political triumph and personal misfortune.

3. One of Kennedy's most famous statements was "Ask not what your country can do for you. Ask what you can do for your country." Discuss how this statement applies to you in relation to your country. What can you do for your country now? What do you hope to do for it in the future?

4. "Kennedy was killed by a lone assassin named Lee Harvey Oswald." State whether you agree or disagree with this statement. Back up your discussion by giving alternate theories of the assassination.

The End of an Empire: Montezuma and Cortes

A. Pre-listening Activities

PREVIEW OF CONTENT

The Aztec Empire of Mexico was one of the most powerful, culturally advanced empires of the fifteenth and sixteenth century world. And yet, in slightly less than two years, this mighty empire was conquered by a small band of treasure-seeking Spanish adventurers. Why did this happen? What factors entered into the downfall of this mighty empire and led to the destruction of such a sophisticated New World culture? In a few minutes we'll take a look at some of the most obvious factors that led to the fall of the great empire of Montezuma.

LECTURE OUTLINE—A TOPIC OUTLINE

I.   Extent and Power of the Aztec Empire
   A. Subjugation of area Indians
   B. Extension of empire from Mexico City to Guatemala
   C. Human sacrifices to Aztec gods
   D. Aztec capital of Tenochtitlan
     1. Largest city in sixteenth-century world
     2. Military fortress
     3. Effective military intelligence system

II. Conquest of Aztec Empire
   A. Forewarning of Spanish invasion
     1. Appearance of white, bearded men
     2. Legend of Aztec god Quetzalcoatl
     3. Cortes thought to be Quetzalcoatl by Montezuma
     4. Spanish gathering of Indian allies
   B. Defeat of the Aztecs
     1. Invasion of the city and capture of the king
     2. Aztec rebellion against the conquerors
     3. Death of Montezuma
     4. Destruction of the capital
     5. Slaughter of the Indians

III. Factors in the Downfall of the Aztecs
   A. Fear of the supernatural
   B. Role of La Malinche, the Indian woman
   C. Cortes's use of Indian allies
   D. Spaniards' superior weaponry
   E. Spaniards' greed

IV. Fusion of Indian and European Cultures Creating the Republic of Mexico

PREVIEW OF VOCABULARY

Fill in the blanks with the appropriate items.

ruins   subjugate   assumes   altar

1. The raised place in a temple, church, or other place of worship on which sacrifices are offered, or at which religious practices are held, is designated an _____ .

2. When one supposes something to be true, or takes something for granted, one _____ something.

3. To conquer by force and to bring under complete control is to _____ .

4. _____ refer to the remains of something that has been destroyed, such as a building, a city, or a temple.

---

military fortress   immobilized   negotiations   prophecy

---

5. To be _____ is to be prevented from taking action on a situation.

6. _____ are discussions for the purpose of reaching an agreement in some matter, such as politics, war, or business.

7. A secure place protected by an army or a band of soldiers is known as a _____ .

8. A _____ is a declaration that an event will happen before it happens or is supposed to happen.

---

intrigue   fusion

---

9. A secret plan of disruption or a program of hostile action revolves around _____ of some kind or other.

10. A combining or union of different elements into a unified whole may be termed a _____ .

CHECK YOUR ANSWERS.

PREVIEW OF SENTENCES

These are some of the sentences that you will hear in the lecture.

1. The Aztecs had *subjugated* and dominated the entire area that is today Mexico City.

2. On the *altars* of the pyramid-temples, thousands of human sacrifices to the Aztec gods were made.

3. The capital city of the Aztec Empire, Tenochtitlan, was a *military fortress* filled with soldiers.

4. Montezuma mistakenly *assumed* that Cortes, the leader of the soldiers of Spain, was the Aztec god, Quetzalcoatl.

5. Cortes founded Mexico City on the *ruins* of the Aztec capital.

6. The *prophecy* of a returning god completely *immobilized* the leader of the Aztec Empire.

7. The Indian woman La Malinche was a great help to Cortes in his *negotiations* with the Indians.

8. The tool of political *intrigue* turned Indian against Indian.

9. After the fall of the Aztec Empire, there was a *fusion* of Indian and European cultures.

B. Listening Activities

LECTURE OVERVIEW

START THE TAPE.

In this presentation as in the previous one, there is no Note-Taking Model for you to follow as you listen to the lecture; however, before you have to listen and take your own notes on the information, I'll first say something about the organization of this lecture on Montezuma and Cortes, and I'll also give you a brief summary of the main points. Be sure to follow the Lecture Outline while you are listening to this Overview.

NOTE-TAKING EXERCISE

As usual before you begin the exercise, you should check the *Word Guide* below. You will, of course, want to abbreviate as many words as often as possible. O.K., let's go on with the lecture and with your note-taking.

Word Guide

(When you use these items in your notes, remember to abbreviate them.) Montezuma / Cortes / the Aztecs / Tenochtitlan / the Gulf Coast / Quetzalcoatl / *La noche triste* / La Malinche / Doña Marina / the Mayan Indians / the Republic of Mexico

_____

_____

_____

_____

_____

_____

_____

_____

_____

_____

_____

_____

MULTIPLE-CHOICE QUESTIONS

In the following exercise, you will hear thirteen questions about the information contained in the lecture. You are to select from the choices (a), (b), (c), or (d) the *correct answer* to the question you have heard.

1. (a) 1403 and 1420
   (b) 1423 and 1440
   (c) 1443 and 1520
   (d) none of the above

2. (a) 30,000
   (b) 60,000
   (c) 330,000
   (d) none of the above

3. (a) 30,000
   (b) 60,000
   (c) 300,000
   (d) 600,000

4. (a) 20 years
   (b) 30 years
   (c) 40 years
   (d) 50 years

5. (a) He gathered together many Indian allies.
   (b) He prepared for war with the Spanish.
   (c) He asked for the advice of La Malinche.
   (d) He allowed the Spaniards to approach his capital.

6. in
   (a) September of 1518
   (b) November of 1519
   (c) June of 1520
   (d) August of 1521

7. in
   (a) June, 1520
   (b) July, 1520
   (c) August, 1520
   (d) September, 1520

8. (a) 40,000
   (b) 46,000
   (c) 52,000
   (d) 58,000

9. (a) 2 months
   (b) 2½ months
   (c) 3 months
   (d) 3½ months

10. (a) 503
    (b) 553
    (c) 5,003
    (d) 5,553

11. (a) He spoke both the Mayan and Aztec languages.
    (b) He was kind to the Indians he met.
    (c) The Aztecs were hated by their Indian neighbors.
    (d) all of the above

12. (a) 553
    (b) 70,000
    (c) 70,553
    (d) 75,000

13. (a) Montezuma's fear of the supernatural
    (b) the advanced weaponry of the Spaniards
    (c) the tool of political intrigue
    (d) all of the above

Check your answers. Then continue working in your book. This is the end of the taped section of Lecture 12.

STOP THE TAPE.

C. Post-listening Activity

TRUE–FALSE STATEMENTS

T = The statement is accurate according to the information presented in the lecture.

F = The statement is inaccurate according to the information presented in the lecture.

? = The accuracy or inaccuracy of the statement cannot be determined from the information presented in the lecture.

1. ____ In the fifteenth century the Aztecs built the most powerful empire ever known.

2. ____ Guatemala was the southern border of the Aztec Empire in the fifteenth century.

3. ____ The Aztecs were opposed to the concept of human sacrifice.

4. ____ Indian prisoners of war were imprisoned somewhere in the pyramid-temples before they were sacrificed.

5. ____ In the 1500s London had about 80 percent fewer people than the Aztec capital had.

6. ____ Montezuma knew that the Spaniards were approaching his capital city long before they ever arrived there.

7. ____ The Spaniards killed most of the Indians they met on their journey to the capital of Tenochtitlan.

8. ____ The Aztecs were a dark-skinned, beardless people.

9. ____ Quite erroneously Montezuma assumed that Cortes was the returning god Quetzalcoatl.

10. ____ The Spaniards sent presents of gold and silver to Montezuma.

11. ____ The Aztecs rebelled seventeen months after their emperor was imprisoned.

12. ____ It is uncertain that Montezuma was killed by his own people.

13. ____ Montezuma received excellent care during his imprisonment.

14. ____ Military superiority benefited the cause of the Indians.

15. ____ Montezuma had prepared for war as soon as he learned of Cortes's arrival in his kingdom.

16. ____ The Aztecs had never seen guns before Cortes's arrival, but they had seen horses before.

17. ____ Many of the non-Aztec Indians rejoiced at the fall of the Aztec Empire.

18. ____ La Malinche spoke Aztec, Mayan, and undoubtedly, Spanish.

19. ____ A small band of only 553 Europeans, alone and single-handedly, brought down the mighty Aztec Empire.

CHECK YOUR ANSWERS.

20. ____ Tenochtitlan was rebuilt within fifty years of its total devastation.

D. Follow-up Activities

TOPICS FOR DISCUSSION OR WRITING

1. In the sixteenth century, Spain brought colonial rule to Mexico. Prepare a written report or an oral discussion about the following:
   a. the foreign influences in your country in the past
   b. the foreign influences in your country today

2. Discuss the roles that the following played in the defeat of the Aztecs by the Spaniards:
   a. superior weaponry
   b. fear of the supernatural
   c. Montezuma's indecisive leadership

3. List several characteristics or traits of the Spanish conquistadors. Use as many descriptive adjectives as possible: for example, many conquistadors were *greedy* men.

4. In Mexico there is a fusion of races, but the country is quite homogeneous in terms of religion and language. Is your country homogeneous or heterogeneous with respect to:
   a. religion?
   b. race?
   c. language?
   d. social customs?
   Explain by giving examples.

Language:
Origin and Diversity

A. Pre-listening Activities

PREVIEW OF CONTENT

It is estimated that the peoples of the world speak about 3,000 different languages. Many of these languages are spoken by only a few hundred or a few thousand people. Others, such as Spanish, English, and Chinese, are used by millions of people. Because of the great number and the great variety of languages in the world, many people have had to learn a "foreign" or second language in order to communicate with those who do not speak their native language. There has even been an attempt to create an artificial "universal" language, called Esperanto, to aid international communication.

In this lecture, the lecturers will take a brief look at some historical facts and at some present-day statistics about one of the most basic forms of our system of communication—language.

LECTURE OUTLINE–A TOPIC OUTLINE

I. Animal and Human Communication Systems
   A. Animal signals
      1. Gestures, sounds, and smells to convey anger, fear, contentment
      2. Inability to carry message beyond immediate situation
   B. Human system of communication—language
      1. Ability to carry messages beyond immediate situation
      2. Multi-dimensional aspects of communication system: speech, writing, sign language, music, dance, painting

II. The Origin of Language
   A. Uncertainty about when, where, and how language began
      1. No written records more than 5,000 years old
      2. Earliest writing done in Sumerian
      3. Uncertainty about whether all modern languages developed from one common source or not
      4. Attempt to trace origin of human languages—comparative linguistics
      5. The tracing of Western languages to the common, unrecorded source—Proto-Indo-European
         a. The major languages of Europe, North and South America
         b. Certain Persian and several of India's chief languages

III. Statistics on Modern Languages
   A. The languages of the Far East family
   B. The languages of the Afro-Asiatic family
   C. Languages spoken by large groups of people today
   D. International languages of today—English and Spanish

IV. The Search for an Artificial "Universal" Language—Esperanto

PREVIEW OF VOCABULARY

Fill in the blanks with the appropriate vocabulary items.

Mesopotamia   code   Sumerian   species

1.   The ancient country of Asia, made up of the region between the lower Tigris and the lower Euphrates rivers is known as _____ .

2.   A group that has certain permanent characteristics in common is termed a _____ .

3.   A _____ is comprised of a system of signals for communication purposes.

4.   _____ was the language of an ancient people who lived in the lower part of Mesopotamia before 3000 B.C.

Proto-Indo-European   prehistory   comparative linguistics

5.   The reconstructed language which was spoken as far back as 4000 B.C. in the eastern part of Europe, probably in the Ukraine, is designated _____ by linguists. No one knows for sure what the structure or vocabulary of the language consisted of since the language was not recorded.

6.   _____ is the study of the similarities and differences among languages.

7.   The history of humankind in the period before written records were kept (before 4000 B.C.) is known as _____ .

lingua franca	Polynesian	Afro-Asiatic family

8. The language family that includes the major languages of northern Africa and the Middle East is called the _____ of languages.

9. _____ is the language of the people who inhabit the islands of Oceania in the central and southeast Pacific Ocean.

10. _____ is the term applied to a language used in common among people who speak different languages; it is an internationally accepted second language.

Esperanto	intrigued	synthetic

11. To be _____ by someone or something is to be extremely interested in or curious about that person or thing.

12. _____ is an artificially constructed language created in 1887. Its vocabulary and grammar are based on the vocabulary and grammar of the major European languages. This _____ or artificial language was devised by a Polish scientist.

CHECK YOUR ANSWERS.

PREVIEW OF SENTENCES

These are some of the sentences that you will hear in the lecture.

1. Both humans and animals communicate with their own *species*.

2. All humans combine sound and meaning into a complex *code* of communication.

3. The oldest known writing was done approximately 5,000 years ago in *Sumerian,* the language of ancient *Mesopotamia*.

4. We do not know whether our different modern languages had one common source or whether they developed from different sources in different places during our *prehistory*.

5. The examination of the similarities and the differences that exist among today's various languages is called *comparative linguistics*.

6. Most of the languages used in the Western world today have been traced to the common, yet unrecorded, source which linguists call *Proto-Indo-European*.

7. There are more speakers of Chinese and *Polynesian* than there are speakers of Russian, Arabic, and the various Western languages put together.

8. Arabic belongs to the *Afro-Asiatic family* of languages.

9. English seems to have replaced French as the world's *lingua franca*.

10. It is no wonder that men and women have been so *intrigued* by the idea of developing an artificial "universal" language.

11. The most well-known attempt to develop an artificial universal language was the development of *Esperanto*.

12. Esperanto is a *synthetic* language which was devised in the nineteenth century by a Polish scientist.

B. Listening Activities

LECTURE OVERVIEW

Just listen and follow the Topic Outline while I give you a brief overview of what will be discussed in this commentary. Since there is no Note-Taking Model, you are asked to listen carefully as I touch upon the various aspects of the origin and diversity of our system of communication—language.

START THE TAPE.

NOTE-TAKING EXERCISE

All right, this is one of the longest lectures you have had to listen to so far. It will require a great deal of concentration on your part to listen to such a long lecture, and it will require skill in note-taking which I hope you're beginning to acquire. Well, let's get started with the exercise. Did you quickly check the *Word Guide*?

Word Guide

Sumerian / Mesopotamian / comparative linguistics / Proto-Indo-European / Chinese / Polynesian / Arabic / Afro-Asiatic / Japanese / French / German / Persian / Vietnamese / *lingua franca* / Esperanto / Dr. L. Zamenhof

_____

_____

_____

_____

_____

_____

_____

_____

_____

_____

_____

_____

_____

_____

_____

MULTIPLE-CHOICE QUESTIONS

In the following exercise, you will hear fifteen questions about the information you heard in the lecture. After hearing the questions, you should look at your paper and select from the choices (a), (b), (c), or (d) the *correct answer* to the question you heard. Certainly refer to your notes before making the choice.

1. (a) gestures
   (b) speech
   (c) writing
   (d) all of the above

2. (a) 5,000 years ago in India
   (b) 15,000 years ago in India
   (c) 25,000 years ago in Mesopotamia
   (d) none of the above

3. by examining
   (a) only the similarities that exist among languages
   (b) only the differences that exist among languages
   (c) the similarities and differences that exist among today's and among ancient languages
   (d) none of the above

4. the major languages of
   (a) Iran
   (b) Europe
   (c) South America
   (d) all of the above

5. (a) 104 million
   (b) 114 million
   (c) 140 million
   (d) none of the above

6. (a) 3.5 million
   (b) 140 million
   (c) 660 million
   (d) 800 million

7. (a) Arabic
   (b) Chinese
   (c) Polynesian
   (d) none of the above

8. (a) 55 million
   (b) 60 million
   (c) 120 million
   (d) none of the above

9. (a) German
   (b) Persian
   (c) Vietnamese
   (d) none of the above

10. (a) 25 million
    (b) 35 million
    (c) 64 million
    (d) none of the above

11. (a) 84 million
    (b) 104 million
    (c) 184 million
    (d) none of the above

12. (a) English
    (b) French
    (c) Spanish
    (d) all of the above

13. (a) Esperanto
    (b) French
    (c) Russian
    (d) none of the above

14. (a) 2,796
    (b) 2,976
    (c) 3,096
    (d) none of the above

15. (a) 13 languages
    (b) 30 languages
    (c) 33 languages
    (d) none of the above

Check your answers. Then continue working in your book. This is the end of the taped section of Lecture 13.

STOP THE TAPE.

C. Post-listening Activity

TRUE–FALSE STATEMENTS

T = The statement is accurate according to the information presented in the lecture.

F = The statement is inaccurate according to the information presented in the lecture.

? = The accuracy or inaccuracy of the statement cannot be determined from the information presented in the lecture.

1. _____ Unlike humans, animals do not communicate with one another.

2. _____ Gorillas will shake their heads from side to side as a warning.

3. _____ Animals are incapable of expressing emotion.

4. _____ Experiments with animals are being conducted to verify the fact that animals use communication signals.

5. _____ In a general sense you are using language when you listen to music and when you go dancing.

6. _____ Writing is the basic form of all language.

7. _____ Oral communication is more prevalent than written communication among humans.

8. _____ There exist today groups of people who have no writing system to record their speech.

9. _____ The origin of language is shrouded in mystery.

10. _____ Uncertainty still prevails today about whether all our languages shared a common source or whether they evolved from different sources in different places.

11. _____ Proto-Indo-European has been designated by linguists as the parent language of all modern languages.

12. _____ Apparently the major languages of Europe, North and South America, Iran, and even of India have all descended from the same language.

13. _____ More people throughout the world speak English as a first language.

14.____ The statistics on the number of speakers of certain languages are accurate and reliable.

15.____ Linguists favor the development of an artificial, "universal" language to replace English.

16.____ At various times in the history of the Eastern world, there have been attempts made to create an artificial "universal" language.

17.____ It is not quite as difficult for a speaker of Arabic or Russian to learn Esperanto as it is to learn English.

CHECK YOUR ANSWERS.

D. Follow-up Activities

TOPICS FOR DISCUSSION OR WRITING

1. Give several reasons why a person who speaks more than one language has a definite advantage over the person who is monolingual.

2. Formulate several reasons why English is used as a common second language by so many people throughout the world.

3. Would it be of great benefit to have people learn and use a universal synthetic language, such as Esperanto? Explain your answer.

4. How do delegates at the United Nations General Assembly communicate with one another?

5. Speculate about which language will be the *lingua franca* in the twenty-first century. Why?

The World's Changing Climate: Fire or Ice?

A. Pre-listening Activities

PREVIEW OF CONTENT

Since the 1940s many unusual changes have been taking place in the world's climate. Some weather scientists are predicting a new "Ice Age," while others are predicting a warming-up period. In either case, the consequences of either trend could be disastrous for human beings.

In this presentation, the lecturers will ask and attempt to answer the following questions:

1. In what ways has the world's climate been changing?
2. What are the two principal hypotheses that climatologists have formed to explain these climatic changes?

3. How have these climatic changes affected various parts of the world?
4. What might be the consequences for humankind if either the warming-up or the cooling-off hypothesis turns out to be true?

LECTURE OUTLINE—A SENTENCE OUTLINE

I. Is the earth cooling off or is it heating up?
   A. Climatologists disagree.
   B. A cooling trend could bring mass starvation and fuel shortages.
   C. A warming trend could bring flooding of the coastal cities.

II. What is happening to global weather conditions?
   A. Africa experienced prolonged drought, followed by rainfall which brought a rat and insect plague.
   B. The continent of Asia is threatened with the disruption of the monsoon pattern.
      1. The summer winds usually blow from the ocean to the continent, bringing moist air and heavy rainfall.
      2. The winter winds usually blow from the continent to the ocean, bringing the dry season to the continent.
      3. If the Asian and North African deserts expand southward (because the earth is cooling off), the monsoon pattern will be disrupted, and droughts will become more frequent occurrences.
      4. In the early 1900s, monsoon winds were penetrating farther north, causing a decline in drought frequency.
      5. Now, the deserts are moving southward and might cause an increase in drought frequency.
   C. Australia has recently been hit by severe drought necessitating the slaughter of livestock.
   D. Europe has undergone abnormal weather conditions. Hotter and drier summers have affected crops, water transportation, and power.
   E. The Midwestern United States has experienced severe drought lately.

III. Is something drastic happening to the global weather systems?
   A. Climatologists disagree.
      1. Higher temperatures might expand the deserts of the world and shorten crop-growing seasons.
      2. Lower temperatures might produce storms, floods, and freezes.

B. Some climatologists believe in the cooling trend.
  1. They predict another "Little Ice Age."
  2. They point to the expanding of the polar ice caps.
  3. They claim the Northern Hemisphere temperature is 1° C (1.8° F) colder.
C. Other climatologists believe in the warming trend.
  1. They cite the increased amount of carbon dioxide in the atmosphere due to pollution as causing a rise in average world temperatures.
  2. They point out that carbon dioxide traps the earth's heat and prevents it from escaping out into space.
D. All climatologists believe the earth's climate is changing and that the change will affect humankind.

B. Listening Activities

PREVIEW OF SENTENCES

START THE TAPE.

Since the following commentary is rather long and detailed, let's preview some of the key sentences in the talk. These sentences will provide a short summary of the lecture content and organization of the talk. They will give you, in other words, a lecture overview. Vocabulary items are not glossed, so if you are not sure of the meaning of a word or phrase, look it up in the dictionary after working through this exercise and before taking notes on the talk. You will be given time to repeat each sentence after you hear it spoken by the lecturers.

1. Climatology, the study of long-range trends in weather, is at best an inexact science.

2. A cooling trend could bring mass starvation and fuel shortages.

3. A warming trend could melt the polar ice caps and cause flooding of the coastal cities of the world.

4. The continent of Africa, up until 1974, had six consecutive years of drought.

5. Along with the rainfall has come a plague of rats, locusts, and caterpillars.

6. The present climatological trend seems to indicate that the monsoon pattern is being disrupted in Asia.

7. In summer, monsoon winds blow from the ocean toward the continent bringing the moist air from the ocean and causing heavy rainfall.

8. In winter, the winds blow from the continent toward the ocean causing the dry season.

9. If the deserts of Asia and North Africa expand and move southward, the monsoons of Asia will be suppressed, and the entire monsoon pattern will be disrupted.

10. The present weather trend seems to be a return to a higher frequency drought pattern for the Asian continent.

11. In the 1976 drought, fodder for cattle was so scarce that Australian farmers killed the livestock they were unable to feed.

12. The climate of Western Europe is also undergoing abnormal conditions.

13. The summer of 1976 was one of Western Europe's hottest and driest.

14. The United States has also been undergoing some major climatic changes that could possibly result in another Dust Bowl for the country.

15. Do all these climatic abnormalities mean that something drastic is happening to the global weather systems?

16. Climatologists, in general, are puzzled by the changes taking place today.

17. A number of climatologists believe the earth is, in fact, undergoing a cooling trend and is returning to the conditions of the "Little Ice Age."

18. Other climatologists believe that the cooling trend is being offset by a warming trend.

19. They believe that this warming trend is being caused by the increase of carbon dioxide in the atmosphere due to pollution from factories, cars, and so forth.

20. We are, indeed, a factor in today's weather equation—a crucial factor with our smog, smoke, and car exhausts.

21. Both groups of climatologists do agree that whatever the long-term trend in the earth's climate is, we are witnessing a period of climatological change.

NOTE-TAKING EXERCISE

All right, now that you have some idea of the main points of the lecture on the world's changing climate, listen to the talk and take notes at the same time. There's a lot of information packed into the lecture, so you will have to concentrate on getting down the gist of the information presented. Certain important details should also be jotted down.

Word Guide

climatology / polar ice caps / gist of the information / cattle / Africa / locusts / caterpillars / Asia / monsoon / Australia / Western Europe / England / France / Belgium / Italy / West Germany / Wisconsin / Little Ice Age

_____

_____

_____

_____

_____

_____

_____

_____

_____

_____

_____

_____

_____

_____

MULTIPLE-CHOICE QUESTIONS

Now you will hear twelve questions about the world's changing climate. After listening to each question, you should select from the choices (a), (b), (c), or (d) the *correct answer* to the question you heard. Be sure that you refer to your notes before making your choice.

1. (a) A plague of rats, locusts, and caterpillars came to the continent.
   (b) Africa had six consecutive years of drought.
   (c) 500,000 people died.
   (d) all of the above

2. (a) summer
   (b) fall
   (c) winter
   (d) spring

3. (a) those regions that are dry half of the year
   (b) those regions that are wet half of the year
   (c) both of the above
   (d) neither of the above

4. (a) one every three or four years
   (b) one every eight years
   (c) one every decade
   (d) one every eighteen years

5. (a) 2,000,000
   (b) 2,001,000
   (c) 2,010,000
   (d) 2,100,000

6. (a) 25%
   (b) 30%
   (c) 66 2/3%
   (d) none of the above

7. (a) 2,000,000 kilos
   (b) 2,000,000 pounds
   (c) 2,000,000 tons
   (d) none of the above

8. (a) $4,000,000
   (b) $40,000,000
   (c) $400,000,000
   (d) $1,400,000,000

9. It was _____ than usual.
   (a) drier
   (b) wetter
   (c) colder
   (d) warmer

10. from the
    (a) 14th century to the 19th century
    (b) 14th century to the mid-19th century
    (c) 19th century to the 20th century
    (d) 19th century to the mid-20th century

11. (a) .56°
    (b) 1.00°
    (c) 1.80°
    (d) 3.60°

12. (a) 10%
    (b) 20%
    (c) 30%
    (d) none of the above

Check your answers. Then continue working in your book. This is the end of the taped section of Lecture 14.

STOP THE TAPE.

C. Post-listening Activity

TRUE–FALSE STATEMENTS

T = The statement is accurate according to the information presented in the lecture.

F = The statement contradicts information presented in the lecture.

? = The accuracy or inaccuracy of the statement cannot be determined from the information presented in the lecture.

1. ____ Climatology is an inexact science because measuring instruments are not exact enough.

2. ____ If the earth heats up, the polar ice caps may constrict.

3. ____ The rain that finally came to Africa was a problem, because it caused flooding of the coastal cities of the continent.

4. ____ In Asia, the present climatological trend seems to indicate that the monsoon pattern is being disrupted in that part of the world.

5. ____ The Asian dry season results from the monsoon winds that blow from the continent toward the ocean.

6. ____ The winter monsoon winds bring the wet season to the continent.

7. ____ If the deserts of North Africa move southward, there will undoubtedly be more droughts in Asia.

8. ____ If the earth does warm up, winds from the ocean will penetrate farther north on the continent.

9. ____ Recently, the continent of Asia has been hit by drought, but the continent of Australia has been plagued by rats and locusts.

10. ____ In the early 1900s, a high drought frequency pattern for Asia resulted because the deserts pushed southward.

11. ____ The climate of Western Europe has been undergoing abnormal weather conditions because of drought and lower temperatures.

12. ____ Food production depends upon the variability of the weather.

13. ____ Climatologists are convinced that something drastic is happening to the earth's global weather conditions.

14. ____ Higher temperatures throughout the world will cause the deserts of the world to shrink.

15. ____ People are affecting the earth's weather dynamics because they are taking more accurate weather measurements.

16. ____ Agricultural planning has become more difficult because the earth is experiencing an era of increasing climatological change.

17. ____ Australian farmers slaughtered an estimated 10,000 head of cattle to prevent the price of beef from falling.

18. ____ The rats and insects brought by the rains have all been destroyed by African farmers.

19. ____ The Asian monsoons penetrate the continent for 5,000 miles.

20. ____ Weather satellites use infra-red film to photograph the north and south poles.

CHECK YOUR ANSWERS.

D. Follow-up Activities

TOPICS FOR DISCUSSION OR WRITING

1. What would be the possible effects of a cooling off of the earth on your country in terms of:
   a. climate?
   b. agriculture?
   c. industry?
   d. occurrence of natural disasters?

2. Discuss the importance of the climatologist to humanity.

3. Synthesize the information contained in the lecture into a short oral or written summary.

4. What can be done to offset the effects of a heating up of the earth due to the increase of carbon dioxide in the earth's atmosphere?

The Egyptian Pyramids: Houses of Eternity

A. Pre-listening Activities

PREVIEW OF CONTENT

The pyramids of ancient Egypt have fascinated and puzzled humanity for centuries. Just how were they built at a time when human beings lacked knowledge of advanced mathematics; when we had no modern machinery or technology; when we had only copper tools to work with? Certain other questions come to mind when trying to understand the incredible mystery of these fantastic monuments; questions such as why would someone—let's say a king—require that 100,000 workers labor for twenty years to construct a tomb to place his dead body in? Was it his attempt to secure immortal life for his soul when his body had stopped functioning? Was it his attempt to hide his possessions from robbers? Was it his fear of being forgotten—of being human rather than superhuman? Or was it his attempt to be equal to an immortal god? To all of these questions, the answer appears to be "yes, indeed."

In the presentation, the lecturers are going to trace the evolution and the development of the pyramid structure, and will attempt to show the human and religious significance of these gigantic monuments to mankind's search for immortality.

LECTURE OUTLINE–A SENTENCE OUTLINE

I. The pyramids of Egypt have survived time and the weather.

II. The pyramids were constructed as burial places for the ancient Egyptian royal family members.
   A. The ancient Egyptians believed in life after death.
      1. They prepared for their afterlife by building tombs (pyramids) and collecting possessions to put into the tombs.
      2. They had their bodies preserved from decay by embalming.
      3. They believed that the dead person could take his or her earthly possessions along to the next world.
   B. The tombs were built to outsmart grave robbers, but almost all of the tombs were broken into and robbed.

III. The structure of the pyramids evolved over the centuries.
   A. The mastaba was constructed during the First and Second Dynasties (3100–2665 B.C.).
   B. The Step Pyramid (the "typical" pyramid) was built during the Third Dynasty (2664–2615 B.C.).
      1. It was built for King Zoser by the architect Imhotep.
      2. It is a pile of mastabas.
      3. King Zoser's step pyramid was never covered with stone to give it a smooth surface.
   C. The pyramids of Giza were built during the Fourth Dynasty (2614–2502 B.C.).
      1. They are located near the town of Giza which is outside Cairo.
      2. They are the best preserved of all the pyramids.
      3. There are three pyramids.
         a. Khufu's (Cheops's) pyramid is the largest.
         b. Khafre's pyramid is smaller.
         c. Mankaure's pyramid is the smallest.

IV.   Construction of pyramids declined after the Fourth Dynasty.
    A. The pyramids offered little or no protection for the dead kings and nobles and for their possessions from grave robbers.
    B. Thutmose I commanded an underground tomb be built far from the Nile River and Cairo (in the Valley of the Kings).
    C. Most pharaohs followed Thutmose's example.

B. Listening Activities

PREVIEW OF SENTENCES

START THE TAPE.

The last commentary in the series deals with the incredible pyramids of Egypt. The discussion is quite long and very involved. To prepare you for the task of listening to a rather long presentation and taking down information on it, you will be given a preview of important points that the speakers highlight in the talk. As you work through these sentences, be sure that you are familiar with the vocabulary that is used. After you listen to each sentence as it is spoken, read and repeat it before you go on to the next one. Some of the sentences are very long, but don't let that alarm you. The first time you hear the sentence, read along. Then try to reconstruct the sentence without looking at the printed word. Concentrate on the meaning of what you hear and read. Don't worry about repeating the sentence word-for-word. Just work on understanding the entirety of the message and then reconstruct as much as you can. O.K. Let's give it a try.

1. Time and weather have been really hard on ancient Egypt's cities and towns, but several of the temples, statues, and, perhaps most important of all, the pyramids have survived.

2. A dynasty is a series of kings or queens of the same royal family.

3. The pyramids were constructed as tombs or burial places for the Egyptian kings and their family members.

4. The Egyptians believed that they could be assured of an afterlife only if their bodies could be preserved from decay or destruction.

5. When a pharaoh died, in order to ensure his eternal life, he had his corpse embalmed or mummified.

6. The ancient Egyptians also believed that the dead person could take along all his earthly possessions to the next world.

7. The grave robbers almost always outsmarted even the most powerful and the most careful of pharaohs.

8. It was during the First and Second Dynasties that the kings and noble persons of Egypt began to construct the type of tomb called the "mastaba."

9. The first "typical" pyramid was built during the Third Dynasty (which lasted roughly from about 2664 until 2615 B.C.).

10. The Step Pyramid was simply a pile of mastabas, each higher step smaller than the one before.

11. It was not until the Fourth Dynasty that the most famous pyramids were built. The three great pyramids of Giza belong to the Fourth Dynasty.

12. It has been estimated that 2,300,000 blocks of limestone were used to build the Great Pyramid.

13. The Great Pyramid of Khufu is considered a wonder of ancient architecture.

14. The ancient Greek historian Herodotus said that 400,000 men worked for twenty years to build the Great Pyramid.

15. The Second and Third Pyramids of Giza were built by Khufu's successors.

16. None of the later pyramids that were built during the next thirteen or fourteen centuries were nearly as large or as magnificent as the Pyramids of Giza.

17. It was becoming increasingly clear to the pharaohs and noble persons of Egypt that the pyramid method of burial provided really very little or no protection at all for their royal corpses.

18. One of the pharaohs, King Thutmose I, decided to sacrifice publicity for safety in the construction of his House of Eternity.

19. Instead of ordering the construction of a pyramid, Thutmose I had his tomb dug out of the rock of a valley far from the Nile River and far from Cairo.

20. After Thutmose I, most of the pharaohs abandoned above-ground pyramid construction in favor of underground hiding places as the burial places for their precious royal bones.

21. The ancient Greeks called the pyramids one of the Seven Wonders of the World.

22. The three mighty Pyramids of Giza, as well as thirty-two other recognizable pyramids, still stand today.

NOTE-TAKING EXERCISE

Well now, you're going to listen to a very long and rather detailed commentary about the pyramids of Egypt. Are you ready to take notes on what you hear? Let's first pause for a moment while you take a look at the *Word Guide*. It includes the names of some ancient Egyptians. Let me pronounce some of them so that you will recognize them when you hear them in the lecture. Look at the *Word Guide*.

Word Guide

King Zoser / Imhotep / Giza—the name of a city in Egypt / King Khufu / Cheops / Napoleon—the French conqueror / Khafre / Mankaure / Thutmose I / Herodotus—the Greek historian

_____

_____

_____

_____

_____

_____

_____

_____

_____

_____

_____

_____

_____

_____

MULTIPLE-CHOICE QUESTIONS

Now you will hear fourteen questions about the information contained in the lecture about the pyramids of Egypt. Some of the questions are quite difficult, so be sure that you have your notes available for consultation. All right, after you hear the question, look at the choices listed in your book. You are to choose from the choices (a), (b), (c), or (d) the *correct answer* to the question you heard. Are you ready?

1. (a) 20 centuries
   (b) 30 centuries
   (c) 40 centuries
   (d) 50 centuries

2. (a) the Mings of China
   (b) the Romanovs of Europe
   (c) the Al-Sauds of Saudi Arabia
   (d) kings and queens of the same royal family

3. (a) wars
   (b) family life
   (c) the afterlife
   (d) affairs of state

4. because if their bodies were destroyed, their souls would
   (a) die
   (b) live forever
   (c) both of the above
   (d) neither of the above

5. (a) the mastaba
   (b) the Step Pyramid
   (c) the Great Pyramid
   (d) the Valley of the Kings tomb

6. B.C.
   (a) 3200–2666
   (b) 3100–2665
   (c) 2664–2615
   (d) 2164–2502

7. in the
   (a) First Dynasty
   (b) Second Dynasty
   (c) Third Dynasty
   (d) Fourth Dynasty

8. (a) Imhotep
   (b) Khufu
   (c) Thutmose
   (d) Zoser

9. (a) 2,300,000
   (b) 2,500,000
   (c) 3,200,000
   (d) 5,200,000

10. meters
    (a) 137
    (b) 147
    (c) 157
    (d) none of the above

11. because
    (a) slaves worked on the pyramid construction
    (b) no modern machinery was used to build it
    (c) no written records about the construction have been found
    (d) the chief architect died before completion of the pyramid

12. (a) 106.2
    (b) 130.6
    (c) 132.6
    (d) none of the above

14. up until
    (a) 3134 B.C.
    (b) 1876 B.C.
    (c) 1786 B.C.
    (d) 1234 B.C.

13. the pyramid of
    (a) Cheops
    (b) Khafre
    (c) Khufu
    (d) Menkaure

STOP THE TAPE. Check your answers. Then continue working in your book. This is the end of the taped section of Lecture 15.

C. Post-listening Activity

TRUE-FALSE STATEMENTS

T = The statement is true.
F = The statement is false.
? = It cannot be determined from the lecture whether the statement is true or false.

1. ____ The civilization of ancient Egypt lasted fewer than 3,000 years.

2. ____ At least thirty dynasties ruled ancient Egypt.

3. ____ The ancient Egyptians believed that if someone's dead body were preserved from decay, his or her soul would cease to exist.

4. ____ In the expression, "You can't take it with you when you go," the "it" referred to a person's material possessions.

5. ____ A pharoah's slaves willingly gave up their lives to serve their master in his afterlife.

6. ____ Grave robbers came from the poorest class of ancient Egyptian society.

7. ____ Grave robbers left poor people's graves undisturbed.

8. ____ The lecturer expressed admiration of the grave robbers when he remarked about their having a grave robbers' union.

9. ____ In shape, a mastaba looks just like a shoe.

10. ____ Zoser and Imhotep are one and the same person.

11. ____ The Pyramid of Cheops and the Pyramid of Khufu were constructed by different architects.

12. ____ Goats, camels, and sheep provided the main meat source for the royal ancient Egyptian diet.

13. ____ The three Great Pyramids were built during the Third Dynasty.

14. ____ The average limestone block used in the Great Pyramid weighed about 15,000 kilos.

15. ____ The top ten meters of the Great Pyramid of Khufu are no longer visible today.

16. ____ The Greek historian Herodotus stated that 100,000 men worked for twenty years to build the Great Pyramid.

17. ____ The Pyramid of Menkaure is the lowest in height of the three Great Pyramids of Giza.

18. ____ Menkaure was a sister of Khafre.

19. ____ Above-ground pyramid building continued for quite a while after Thutmose I's reign.

20. ____ The ancient Egyptian pharaohs were enormously powerful and obsessed people.

CHECK YOUR ANSWERS.

D. Follow-up Activities

TOPICS FOR DISCUSSION OR WRITING

1. Trace the evolution of the pyramid structure. (Refer to the lecture script.)

2. Explain why King Thutmose I decided not to be buried in a pyramid.

3. Compare and contrast your view of life-after-death with those of the ancient Egyptians.

4. Using a reference such as an encyclopedia, give a detailed oral or written report on one of the following:
   a. the mastaba pyramids
   b. the Step Pyramids
   c. the Pyramid of Cheops

5. Report orally or in writing about the discovery of the tomb of the boy pharaoh, King Tutankhaman.

6. The construction of pyramids was an example of the search for life everlasting. Why and in what other ways have people searched for immortality?

Appendix
Scripts and Answer Keys

LECTURE 1 MODEL

The United Nations: The Promise of Peace

The United Nations, as most of you already know, is an organization of 141 countries. This is according to the latest figures. The purpose of the United Nations Organization—at least the original purpose of the U.N.—is to maintain international peace and to promote international cooperation among nations. Its *headquarters* is in the United States, in New York City, but there are branches of the U.N. in Paris, in Rome, and in Geneva.

It was back in 1944 that the United Nations was first planned. In that year, representatives of twenty-six countries *pledged* that their governments would continue to fight against Germany and Italy in World War II. The *charter* of the U.N. was formally signed by fifty countries in October of 1945 in San Francisco, California.

In 1950 John D. Rockefeller, Jr., the well-known millionaire and *philanthropist,* gave the United Nations Organization a section of land in New York City. The United States government then *lent* the U.N. $65 million to construct a building on this land to house the international organization. Today, the U.N. occupies 73 hectares—or 18 acres, as we say in the U.S.—right in the heart of New York City; right in the center of the city. The United Nations *budget* now totals more than $450 million per year. According to a recent statistic, the United States contributed 25 percent of the total U.N. budget; the Soviet Union contributed 12.9 percent, and Japan was the third largest contributor with 7.15 percent. 5.86 percent of the budget was covered by France.

We aren't going to discuss the structure of the United Nations Organization at this time, but let me just add one final comment. When a country joins the U.N., it promises to settle any dispute or disagreement it has with another country peacefully. This is a promise that's not always easy to keep, but it's certainly one that is so vital, so really necessary, in this day of world-wide *nuclear weapons.*

SCRIPT

LECTURE 1 NOTE-TAKING EXERCISE

The United Nations, as most of you perhaps already know, is an organization of 141 countries. This is according to the latest figures.

How much of what you just heard was important enough to include in your notes? Really only the words—the United Nations; 141 countries. Did you write these down? Good. Let's go on with the lecture.

The purpose of the United Nations Organization—at least the original purpose of the U.N.—is to maintain international peace and to promote international cooperation among nations.

Did you reduce what you heard to five or six key words? What were they? Did you notice that the lecturer repeated some words? Listen again to the sentence. Which words are repeated? Write them down.

The purpose of the United Nations Organization—at least the original purpose of the U.N.—is to maintain international peace and to promote international cooperation among nations.

The repeated words were: purpose, U.N., international.
Why would you not write the words that were repeated in your notes?
Let's go back to the lecture.

The United Nations headquarters is in the United States, in New York City, but there are branches of the U.N. in Paris, in Rome, and in Geneva.

Look at what you wrote. Did you put down the following words: headquarters, New York City, branches, Paris, Rome, Geneva? Did you remember to abbreviate some of these words? You might have abbreviated the words Paris, Rome, and Geneva. If you did, are you sure that you would know that P meant Paris, and not Prague? And that R meant Rome, and not Riyadh? You must be sure when you are using abbreviations that they are meaningful when you look at them at a later time. This is why they were not abbreviated in the Note-Taking Model. However, there were several words that certainly should have been abbreviated. What were they? They were headquarters—hdqtr; New York City—NYC; and branches—branch.
Now let's listen to several sentences from the lecture. Take notes as you listen. Ready?

It was in 1944 that the United Nations was first planned. In that year, representatives of twenty-six countries pledged that their governments would continue to fight against Germany and Italy in World War II. The charter of the U.N. was formally signed by fifty countries in October of 1945 in San Francisco, California. Fifty countries signed in October, 1945, in San Francisco, California.

Did you get down all the facts? Check your notes, and see if you can answer these questions. When was the U.N. first planned? Did twenty-six or thirty-six countries pledge to continue to fight Germany and Italy? How many countries formally signed the U.N. charter in California? In what year was the U.N. charter formally signed?

If you took down all the information as you listened to the lecture, you should have been able to look at your notes and answer these questions. Check your answers. "When was the U.N. first planned?" Looking at your notes, you should have found that it was in 1944. The answer to the second question, "Did twenty-six or thirty-six countries pledge to continue to fight Germany and Italy?," is 26—two six. The answer to the third question, "How many countries formally signed the U.N. charter in California?," is 50—five zero. And the answer to the last question, "In what year was the U.N. charter formally signed?," is 1945—one nine four five. Later in the book, you will be asked to answer many questions about the information you hear in the lectures. You will also have a chance to look at your notes for the answers to the questions. So, if you take good notes, you should be able to answer the questions. Now let's get back to the lecture. Are you ready to take notes? Some of the information will be repeated.

In 1950 John D. Rockefeller, Jr., the well-known oil millionaire and philanthropist, gave the United Nations a section of land in New York City. The United States government then lent the U.N. Organization $65 million, $65 million, to construct a building on this land to house the international organization. Today, the U.N. occupies 73 hectares,—or 18 acres, as we say in the U.S.—right in the heart of New York City; that's right in the center of the City.

Check your notes for a minute. Did you have time to write down all the facts? You should have. Do you think it was important to write down John D. Rockefeller's name accurately? Not really. You should have made some attempt at it, but you can always check the spelling of a name or the accuracy of other details when the lecture or class is over. Students should not be afraid to ask questions after class if they did not understand what the professor said.

Listen now as the lecturer discusses the United Nations budget. Take notes as you listen.

The United Nations budget now totals more than $450 million per year. According to a recent statistic, the United States contributed 25 percent of the total U.N. budget, the Soviet Union, or Russia, contributed 12.9 percent, and Japan was the third largest contributor with 7.15 percent. 5.86 percent of the budget was covered by France.

Numbers are not always easy to understand. And numbers with decimal points are even more difficult to understand and write down. Did you write down the following information: the budget—$450 million (dollar sign four five zero million)? It would have taken too long to write out the entire number, so you could *have used the small letter m to indicate the million number. Did you write down the U.S. two five percent? Russia, one two point nine percent? Japan, seven point one five percent, and France, five point eight six percent? Did you get all these figures? Did you use the symbol for the word percent?*

Now let's listen as the lecturer finishes her discussion of the U.N. Are you ready to take notes again?

We aren't going to discuss the structure of the United Nations Organization at this time, but let me just add one final comment. When a country joins the U.N., it promises to settle any dispute or disagreement it has with another country peacefully. This is a promise that's not always easy to keep, but it is certainly one that is so vital, so really necessary, in this day of world-wide nuclear weapons.

How many facts or how much important information was contained in what the lecturer just said? Really, not that much. Lecture language is full of phrases like "let me add one final comment"; of course, they don't have to be written down in your notes. The expression just lets the student know that the lecture is coming to an end. Did you also notice that the lecturer repeated or, really, further explained that it was so vital, so really necessary, to settle disputes peacefully? This is also quite typical of lecturers. They repeat themselves a lot, or they use other words to say what they said previously. You will learn to ignore (for purposes of note-taking) the repetitions of ideas or phrases.

The lecture will now be given again without interruptions. You should be familiar enough with the information and vocabulary that you can concentrate on developing your note-taking style. Are you ready? Listen to the lecture and take notes. Pretend that you are listening to an actual classroom lecture.

Key to Preview of Vocabulary (Lecture 1)

1. headquarters
2. pledge
3. charter
4. lend
5. philanthropist
6. budget
7. nuclear weapons

LECTURE 2 MODEL

The Weather: Meteorology and Meteorologists

We often hear the expression, "Everybody talks about the weather, but nobody does anything about it." This is really not true today. Something is, indeed, being done. Today, *meteorology* is used to make people's lives safer and better. *Meteorologists* are constantly studying the weather. Some meteorologists observe the weather, others analyze weather information, and still others *make forecasts* about the weather. Many forecasts help to *warn* people of approaching bad weather and storms.

The United States National Weather Service operates a *network* of weather stations throughout the U.S. The Weather Service has more than 400 stations where information about the weather is collected and recorded. At these stations, weather observations are taken every hour, both during the day and at night. The Weather Service issues twenty-four-hour weather forecasts. It also issues five-day forecasts and even thirty-day forecasts. It may seem hard to believe, but some types of weather forecasts are 95 percent accurate.

In the year 1959, the United States *launched* its first weather *satellite*. This satellite was specifically designed to collect, record, and send back weather information to earth. Since that time, several weather satellites have been sent into space. They continue to provide valuable weather information to meteorologists in all parts of the world.

Accurate weather forecasts can save thousands of lives and millions of dollars in property damage. Meteorology is, indeed, helping to make our lives safer and better.

LECTURE 2 NOTE-TAKING EXERCISE

We often hear the expression, "Everybody talks about the weather, but nobody does anything about it." This is really not true today. Something is, indeed, being done. Today, meteorology is used to make people's lives safer and better. Meteorologists are constantly studying the weather.

Now, let's check your notes. How much of the information you just heard was worth writing down in your notes? Not much really. The lecturer began with a short introduction to the topic of weather and the science of studying the weather—meteorology. This was just an introduction to the lecture and did not have to be written down as notes. Perhaps the only notable information was the statement that meteorology is used to make people's lives safer and better and that meteorologists are constantly studying the weather. Did you write down this information in your notes? O.K. Let's get back to the lecture.

Some meteorologists observe the weather, others analyze weather information, and still others make forecasts about the weather. Many forecasts help to warn people of approaching bad weather and storms.

O.K. Did you get a chance to note down that some meteorologists observe; others analyze; while others forecast the weather? I hope you abbreviated the word meteorologists. Did you also note down that forecasts warn of approaching storms? Good. Did you also use the "ditto mark" in your notes to save time in note-taking? Fine. Let's go on then.

The United States National Weather Service operates a network of weather stations throughout the U.S. The Weather Service has more than 400 stations where information about the weather is collected and recorded. The Weather Service has 400 stations to collect and read information. At these stations, weather observations are taken every hour, both during the day and at night. Weather observations are taken hourly, day and night. The Weather Service issues twenty-four-hour weather forecasts. It also issues five-day forecasts and even thirty-day forecasts. It may seem hard to believe, but some types of weather forecasts are 95 percent accurate.

That's twenty-four-hour forecasts, five-day forecasts, and thirty-day forecasts. Some of these forecasts are 95 percent accurate. Did you get down these facts? I hope you didn't worry about the spelling of the word "accurate." O.K. Let's go on.

In the year 1959, the United States launched its first weather satellite. This satellite was specifically designed to collect, record, and send weather information back to earth. Since that first weather satellite of 1959, several other weather satellites have been sent into space. They continue to provide valuable weather information to meteorologists in all parts of the world.

Accurate weather forecasts can save thousands of lives and millions of dollars in property damage. Meteorology is, indeed, helping to make our lives safer and better. Let me repeat that accurate weather forecasts or predictions can save thousands of lives, and they can save millions of dollars in property damage.

Did you use symbols when you were writing down this information? You certainly should have used symbols and abbreviations. They save time when taking down information.

Did you note down the year in which the U.S. sent its first weather satellite into space? What was the satellite specifically designed to do? Did you also jot down that other weather satellites have been launched since the first one was? If you were asked the question: "Why are accurate weather forecasts valuable?" could you locate the answer to the question in your notes? If so, then you're doing just fine.

Now let's see if you can answer a few more questions on the lecture. You will need to look at your notes to find the answers to some of the questions.

Key to Preview of Vocabulary (Lecture 2)

1. warn
2. make forecasts
3. meteorology
4. satellite
5. launched
6. network

Key to Multiple-Choice Questions (Lecture 2)

1. How many weather stations does the U.S. Weather Service operate?   (c)
2. What kinds of weather forecasts does the Weather Service issue?   (c)
3. How accurate are some types of forecasts?   (d)
4. When did the U.S. launch its first weather satellite?   (c)
5. What do weather satellites do?   (c)

Key to True–False Statements (Lecture 2)

1. F   Everybody talks about the weather, but nobody does anything about it.
2. T
3. F   Weather forecasts help to warn people of approaching *bad* weather.
4. F   The U.S. National Weather Service operates a system of weather stations *in the United States.*
5. T
6. T
7. F   The U.S. launched its first *weather* satellite in 1959.
8. F   Since the first weather satellite of 1959, several other weather satellites have been sent into space.
9. T
10. F   *Accurate,* not inaccurate, weather forecasts can save thousands of lives and millions of dollars in property damage.

Key to 30-Day Weather Report for the Continental United States

1. The states of California, Arizona, and Maine will have warmer than usual temperatures.
2. Florida will have cooler temperatures than usual.
3. The Northeast of the country will receive more rainfall than usual.
4. The northwestern tip of California will receive a lesser amount of precipitation than it normally does.
5. Temperatures will be below normal in the American Midwest.
6. The U.S. will experience colder and wetter weather during this 30-day period.
7. The Northern Midwest should be drier than usual.
8. The Northwest of the country should be cooler than usual.

LECTURE 3 MODEL

The Grand Canyon: One of Nature's Finest Monuments

SCRIPT

One of the most *spectacular* sights in the entire United States is the Grand Canyon of the Colorado River. Each year thousands of people visit northern Arizona to see it. Actually the Grand Canyon is really a huge *gorge* cut by the Colorado River. Let's talk about its dimensions for a minute. The gorge itself is 217 miles long, and it is more than one mile deep. It varies in width from four to eighteen miles. The area around the Canyon averages between 5,000 and 10,000 feet in height. The north *rim* of the Canyon is 1,000 feet higher than the south rim. So the north rim has much colder temperatures than the south rim does.

As for the amount of rainfall in the Grand Canyon, the north rim has an average annual rainfall of about twenty-six inches while the south rim has only about sixteen inches. On the floor of the Canyon, there is less than ten inches of rainfall in a year.

As I said before, the Canyon walls were cut by the Colorado River, and they hold a long record of *geologic change.* You can see many plant and animal *fossils* in these walls. Today, plant and animal life in the Canyon is quite *abundant* and varied. The Grand Canyon Park contains 1,000 kinds of plants, more than 200 species or varieties of birds, and about sixty-seven species of *mammals.*

The first Europeans to see the Canyon were Spaniards. They were members of Coronado's *expedition* of 1540. These first European visitors were guided by *Hopi* Indians. Today, Indians occupy much of the land around the Grand Canyon. The *Navajo* Indians live on a 15,000,000-acre *reservation* just east of the Park. In the center of the Navajo Reservation lies the 631,000-acre Hopi Indian reservation. About 200 *Havasupai* Indians live on a small 518-acre reservation near the Canyon.

In the year 1919, President Woodrow Wilson established the Grand Canyon National Park in order to protect and preserve the Park's land and wildlife. President Wilson said that the Grand Canyon was the one sight that every American should see. Today, many Americans and many foreigners visit the Grand Canyon—one of Nature's finest monuments.

LECTURE 3 NOTE-TAKING EXERCISE

One of the most spectacular sights in the entire United States is the Grand Canyon of the Colorado River. Each year thousands of people visit northern Arizona to see the Grand Canyon. Actually, the Grand Canyon is really a huge gorge—or deep valley—which was cut by the Colorado River. Now let's talk about its dimensions for a minute. The gorge itself is 217 miles long, and it is more than one mile deep. It varies in width from four to eighteen miles. The area around the Canyon averages between 5,000 and 10,000 feet in height. The north rim of the Canyon is 1,000 feet higher than the south rim. So as you might expect, the north rim of the Canyon has much colder temperatures than the south rim does.

SCRIPT

Now check your notes. Did you write down the following information? It's in northern Arizona. It's 217 miles long. It is more than one mile deep and is from four to eighteen miles wide. The area averages between 5,000 feet and 10,000 feet in height. The north rim of the Canyon is 1,000 feet higher than the south rim. Did you get this down? All right, let's get back to the lecture.

Now, as for the amount of rainfall in the Grand Canyon region, the north rim of the Canyon has an average rainfall of about twenty-six inches while the south rim of the Canyon has only about sixteen inches of rainfall. On the floor of the Canyon, there is less than ten inches of rainfall in a year.

Did you catch that? The north rim—about twenty-six inches, the south—about sixteen inches. On the Canyon floor, less than ten inches of rainfall in a year. Fine. Let's continue.

As I said before, the Canyon walls were cut by the Colorado River, and these walls hold a long record of geologic change. You can actually see many plant and animal fossils in these walls. You can really see the remains of plants and animals in these walls. Today, plant and animal life in the Canyon is quite abundant and varied. Let me give you an example. The Grand Canyon Park contains about 1,000 kinds of plants, more than 200 species or varieties of birds, and about sixty-seven species of mammals.

Let me give those numbers again. That's about 1,000 kinds of plants, more than 200 species of birds . . . sixty-seven species of mammals.

The first Europeans to see the Grand Canyon were Spaniards. They were Spaniards. They were members of Coronado's expedition of 1540. That's spelled C–o–r–o–n–a–d–o—Coronado's expedition of 1540. These first Europeans were guided to the Canyon by Hopi Indians (H–o–p–i Indians). Today, Indians occupy a lot of the land around the Grand Canyon. In fact, the Navajo Indians live on a 15,000,000-acre reservation just east of the Park. In the center of the Navajo reservation there's the 631,000-acre Hopi Indian reservation. In addition to this, about 200 Havasupai Indians live on a small 518-acre reservation near the Canyon. Havasupai is spelled H–a–v–a–s–u–p–a–i.

Check your notes again. The Navajos—on a 15,000,000-acre reservation; the Hopis—on a 631,000-acre reservation; and 200 Havasupais have a 518-acre reservation.

In the year 1919, in 1919, the American president Woodrow Wilson established the Grand Canyon National Park in order to protect and preserve the Park's land and its wildlife. President Wilson said that the Grand Canyon was the one sight that every American should see. Today, many Americans and many foreigners visit the Grand Canyon which is truly one of Nature's finest monuments.

How did you manage with your note-taking? Did you catch the date the American president established the Grand Canyon National Park? Why did he do this? Right, it was to protect the Park's land and wildlife. Fine. Now get ready for a quiz on the lecture information.

Key to Preview of Vocabulary (Lecture 3)

1. fossils
2. Navajo, Hopi, Havasupai
3. expedition
4. rim
5. spectacular
6. gorge

7. geologic
8. reservations
9. mammals
10. abundant

Key to Multiple-Choice Questions (Lecture 3)

1. How many miles long is the Grand Canyon?   (b)
2. How many miles wide is the Grand Canyon at its widest point?   (b)
3. How many more inches of rainfall does the north rim of the Canyon get than the south rim does?   (a)
4. What can be seen in the walls of the Grand Canyon?   (b)
5. How many kinds of plants can be found in the Grand Canyon Park?   (d)
6. How many more species of birds than mammals are there in the Grand Canyon Park?   (b)
7. In what year did the first Europeans see the Grand Canyon?   (d)
8. Which group of Indians occupies the largest amount of land in the Grand Canyon area?   (b)
9. How many acres of land do the Hopi Indians occupy?   (d)
10. How many Havasupai Indians live near the Grand Canyon?   (a)

Key to True–False Statements (Lecture 3)

1. F   It is *217* miles long
2. F   It is four to eighteen miles *wide.*
3. T
4. F   The *north* rim gets twenty-six inches of rain, while the south rim gets sixteen inches.
5. T
6. F   There is a long record of *geologic* (not geographic) change in the walls of the Grand Canyon.
7. T
8. F   They were guided by *Hopi* Indians.
9. F   They saw it in 1540—which is in the *sixteenth* (not the fifteenth) century.
10. T
11. T
12. F   He established the Grand Canyon National Park in the early twentieth century—in 1919.

Key to Writing Exercise (Lecture 3)

Possible answers:
1. The area around the Canyon averages between 5,000 and 10,000 feet in height.
2. The north rim of the Canyon is 1,000 feet higher than the south rim.
3. The Grand Canyon Park contains 1,000 kinds of plants, and more than 200 species of birds.
4. In 1919 President Woodrow Wilson established the Grand Canyon National Park to protect the animals and land.
5. The first Europeans to see the Grand Canyon were Spaniards. They were members of Coronado's expedition.

LECTURE 4 MODEL

Japan: Industrial Giant of the Far East

SCRIPT

Japan is an island country in the Pacific Ocean. As the Japanese students already know, four main islands and more than 3,000 small ones stretch from north to south for about 1,300 miles. As for the climate of the country, well, it's hot and humid in the summer, but it is quite cold and wet in Japan during the winter. Typhoons, which are violent tropical storms, often *threaten* Japan during the fall. That's, of course, during the harvest season.

The population of Japan is about 110½ million. It may seem hard to believe, but the average *population density* of the country is about 678 persons per square mile. Just in comparison, let me point out that the average population density of the United States was recently listed at fifty-seven persons per square mile. About two thirds of the entire population lives in Japan's cities. The other one third lives in the suburbs or in the rural areas. As a matter of fact, no other country in southern or eastern Asia has such a large urban, or city, population. Tokyo, the capital city of Japan, is the most densely-populated city in the world. At last count there were more than 11.5 million people living in Tokyo. Just imagine, 11.5 million people!

Let me *cite* a few other problems facing Japan today. I'll start with the problem of her natural resources. Japan has a wide variety of resources, but their quantity is really very small. There's gold, copper, silver, and so on, but, as I said, there isn't much of these minerals. So Japan must import most of its minerals. Japan must also import large quantities of food and *raw materials*. And in order to pay for these goods, the Japanese export products that they manufacture, such as TVs, cars, and so forth. Since World War II, Japan has become one of the world's chief industrial and manufacturing countries. In fact, it now has the highest standard of living in all Asia. I must again point out, however, that Japan's amazing economic and industrial growth has brought problems as well as *prosperity* to the country; industrial pollution and *inflation* are major problems for Japan today. And yet, in spite of these economic and environmental problems, Japan enjoys a high standard of living, as I said before.

O.K. Let me get away from talking about Japan's problems now so I can tell you a few things about Japanese education and culture. First of all, to the Japanese *literacy* is a necessity rather than a *luxury*. So more than 95 percent of the Japanese people are literate. It is required that all Japanese children attend school for at least nine years—for six years of elementary school and for three years of junior high school. They may attend senior high school and the university if they pass the difficult entrance examinations for each.

As many people are aware, respect for learning and tradition and a love of beauty are traditional Japanese characteristics. The Japanese often express this love of beauty in the creation and enjoyment of beautiful art, sculpture, *ceramics,* music, and theater productions.

It is well known that the Japanese try to combine the best of the Japanese and Western ways of life. The people eat both Japanese and Western food. They read Japanese and Western books, and they wear Japanese and Western clothing. They also listen to both Oriental and Western music. They say both the Oriental and the Westerner can feel quite at home in the capital city of Tokyo.

Although they are a very industrious, hard-working, and *enterprising* people, which is, of course, reflected in the growth and strength of their economy, the Japanese still manage to enjoy their *leisure time.* They really enjoy sports, such as soccer, swimming, judo, *wrestling,* karate, and baseball. They also like to take vacation trips both in their own country and abroad.

LECTURE 4 NOTE-TAKING EXERCISE

Japan is an island country in the Pacific Ocean. As the Japanese students already know, four main islands and more than 3,000 small ones stretch from north to south for about 1,300 miles. As for the climate of the country, well, it's hot and humid in the summer, but it is quite cold and wet during the winter. Typhoons, which are violent tropical storms, often threaten Japan during the fall. That's, of course, during the harvest season.

SCRIPT

O.K., let's check your notes. Did you take down the information that: 1. Japan is in the Pacific Ocean.   2. There are four main islands and more than 3,000 small ones that stretch for about 1,300 miles.   3. It's hot and wet in the summer; cold and wet in the winter. Typhoons threaten Japan in the fall.

These are the facts. Did you take them down? You heard the lecturer use the expression: "As the Japanese students already know . . ." I hope you did not try to take this down in your notes. The lecturer was just interjecting a personal remark into his talk.

All right. Let's continue the lecture.

The population of Japan is about 110½ million. It may seem hard to believe, but the average population density is about 678 persons per square mile. Just in comparison, let me point out that the average population density of the United States was recently listed at fifty-seven persons per square mile. About two thirds of the entire population of Japan lives in its cities. The other one third of the population lives in the suburbs or in the rural areas. As a matter of fact, no other country in southern or eastern Asia has such a large urban, or city, population. Tokyo, the capital city of Japan, is the most densely-populated city in the world. At last count there were more than 11.5 million people living in Tokyo. Just imagine, 11.5 million people!

Now, check your notes for a minute. Population—110½ million. Did you abbreviate the word million? It would have taken too long to write out all the zeros in the figure, so abbreviating the word was quicker. Population density of Japan—678 persons per square mile; the U.S.—fifty-seven persons. Two thirds of the population lives in the cities. One third lives in the suburbs. Tokyo—the most densely-populated city in the world. 11.5 million people in Tokyo. How are you doing so far? Let's continue taking notes.

Let me cite a few other problems facing Japan today. I'll start with the problem of her limited natural resources. Japan has a wide variety of minerals, but their quantity is quite small. There's gold and copper, silver, and so on, but as I said there isn't much of these minerals. So Japan must import most of these minerals. Japan must also import large quantities of food and raw materials. And in order to pay for these goods, the Japanese must export products that they manufacture, such as TVs, cars, and so on. Let me reiterate: Japan has a variety but a small quantity of these minerals so it must import minerals, food, and raw materials, and export manufactured products. Since the war, Japan has become a chief industrial country.

It's a fact that Japan now has the highest standard of living in all Asia. I should point out, however, that Japan's amazing economic and industrial growth has brought problems as well as prosperity to the country; industrial pollution and inflation are major problems for Japan today. Yes, Japan has the highest standard of living in Asia, but it also has industrial pollution and inflation problems.

In spite of these economic and environmental problems, Japan enjoys a high standard of living, as I said before.

Let's check that you noted down that Japan has a variety but small amount of minerals like gold, silver, and copper, so it imports food and raw materials and exports manufactured goods, and that it's a chief industrial country that has the highest living standard in Asia—not necessarily in the whole world, but certainly in Asia. Did you also jot down the words "problems"; "pollution"; "inflation"; and "high standard of living"? Did you use the chemical symbols for the minerals mentioned? O.K. Great.

Let me get away from talking about Japan's problems now so I can tell you a few things about Japan's education and culture. First of all, to the Japanese literacy is a necessity rather than a luxury. Literacy is a necessity, not a luxury. More than 95 percent of the Japanese people are able to read and write. More than 95 percent are literate. It is required that all Japanese children attend school for at least nine years—for six years of elementary school and for three years of junior high school. They may attend senior high school and the university *if* they pass the difficult entrance examinations for each.

Did you get that down? Check your notes.

As many people are aware, respect for learning and tradition and a love of beauty are traditional Japanese characteristics. The Japanese often express this love of beauty in the creation and enjoyment of beautiful art, sculpture, ceramics, music, and theater productions. I'll repeat that for your notes. They create beautiful art, sculpture, ceramics, music, and theater productions.

It is well-known that the Japanese try to combine the best of the Japanese and Western ways of life. The people eat both Japanese and Western food. They read Japanese and Western books, and they wear Japanese and Western clothing. They also listen to both Oriental and Western music. They say both the Oriental and the Westerner can feel quite at home in the capital city of Tokyo.

Did you write down that they combine Japanese and Western food, books, clothing, and music, and that Tokyo has an Oriental and Western flavor to it? Good.

Although they are a very industrious, hard-working, and an enterprising people, which is, of course, reflected in the growth and strength of their economy, the Japanese still manage to enjoy their leisure time. They really enjoy sports, such as soccer, swimming, judo, wrestling, karate, and baseball. And of course, they also like to take vacation trips both in their country and abroad.

All right. Let's see how you're developing your ability to listen to a lecture and take notes on the information contained in the lecture. You should be feeling more confident about taking notes in English. So let's have a quiz on the information you learned about Japan. You should have your notes ready to help you answer the questions.

Key to Preview of Vocabulary (Lecture 4)

1. leisure time
2. literacy
3. ceramics
4. raw materials
5. enterprising

6. threaten
7. wrestling
8. cite
9. luxury
10. inflation
11. population density
12. prosperity

Key to Multiple-Choice Questions (Lecture 4)

1. How many miles long is the country of Japan?   (c)
2. What is the population of Japan?   (c)
3. How many more people per square mile are there in Japan than in the United States?   (c)
4. What percentage of the Japanese population lives in the suburbs or rural areas?   (c)
5. What must Japan import because of its limited natural resources?   (b)
6. What has resulted from Japan's amazing economic growth?   (d)
7. How many years of junior high school must Japanese children attend?   (a)
8. How do the Japanese try to combine the Oriental and Western ways of life?   (d)
9. What kind of music do the Japanese listen to?   (d)
10. Which sport was not mentioned by the lecturer?   (d)

Key to True–False Statements (Lecture 4)

1. F   It is 1,300 miles *long*.
2. T
3. F   It has brought *problems* as well as prosperity.
4. T
5. T
6. F   Japan has a large variety of minerals, but their quantity is quite *small*.
7. F   They enjoy the highest standard of living in *Asia*.
8. F   They are required to attend junior high school. They attend senior high school if they can pass the entrance examination.
9. T
10. T

LECTURE 5 MODEL

Kuwait: Pipeline of the Middle East

SCRIPT

    Kuwait is a country which is quite small, but which is very rich. It has a population of a little more than a million, and it is situated at the north end of the Arabian Gulf, which is also sometimes called the Persian

Gulf. As I just said, Kuwait is a small country. Its land area is about 8,000 square miles, or in metric terms, that's about 2,000,000 hectares. Kuwait's climate is one of the hottest in the world. Let me give you an example of the range in temperatures: in the summer, the temperature often reaches 124° Fahrenheit during the day. That's about 51.1° on the Centigrade scale. Temperatures are naturally cooler during the winter. They range between 50° and 60° Fahrenheit. In other words, they range between 10° and 15.5° Celsius.

Until oil was discovered there in 1938, Kuwait was a little-known country which was ruled by an Arab *sheikh.* Today this small desert country has become one of the world's leading oil producers; it has approximately 15 percent of the world's known *petroleum reserves.*

Since the discovery of oil, Kuwait's rulers have turned the country into a *prosperous* welfare state. It has free primary and secondary education, free health care and social services; and the Kuwaitis do not have to pay any personal *income tax* for those services. I might just add that, in terms of national income *per capita,* Kuwait is one of the world's wealthiest nations. The per capita income was listed in the late '70s as $11,431 per person. That's about 3,184 Dinars, as the Kuwaiti currency is called. As I mentioned before, Kuwait has free primary and secondary education for its people. The rate of literacy is high and constantly growing. The University of Kuwait was opened in 1966, but many of the Kuwaiti students still study in colleges and universities abroad, at state expense, I might add.

I want to talk about the population of the country for a minute. Kuwait is, needless to point out, an Arab country, and about 99 percent of the people who live there are Moslems. That is, they follow the teachings of the prophet Mohammed. And yet, it is interesting to note that fewer than half of these Moslems are actually citizens of Kuwait. This is because there are many Moslem immigrants living and working there. Many of these recent immigrants have come from all over the Arab world—from places like Egypt, Syria, Lebanon, from Oman, and from the Sudan. Indians, Pakistanis, and Iranians live and work in Kuwait, too. The other 1 percent of the population, in other words the non-Moslems, are recent immigrants who were attracted by the opportunities to work for the oil companies. There are several thousand Europeans and Americans in Kuwait. Many of them, as you might imagine, are employed by the oil companies.

Until the discovery of oil, most of the people in Kuwait lived in the traditional fashion. What I mean by this is that the people who lived in the old, walled town of Kuwait lived in simple, mud and brick houses. The people who lived outside the town were *Bedouin nomads,* and these Bedouins made their living raising camels, goats, and sheep. But today, almost all of the old, walled town is gone. It has been replaced by Kuwait City, which is a modern urban center.

On June 19, 1961, Kuwait gained its independence. Today, Kuwait, like England, is a *constitutional monarchy* whose head of state is the *Emir.*

The Emir is chosen for life from the Sabah family by members of the family. This royal *dynasty* has ruled the country for over two hundred years. It was founded in the year 1756. Today, the Emir exercises *executive power* through a Prime Minister, a Council of fifteen members, and a National Assembly. The National Assembly's fifty members are elected by the citizens of Kuwait and serve for four-year terms. Naturally, only the citizens of Kuwait are permitted to vote, that is, to participate in the country's politics; but let me say that all Kuwaiti residents—citizen or recent immigrant, Moslem or non-Moslem—do benefit from the country's free social services and from its wealth.

LECTURE 5 NOTE-TAKING EXERCISE

SCRIPT   Kuwait is a country which is quite small, but which is very rich. It has a population of a little more than a million, and it is situated at the north end of the Arabian Gulf, which is also sometimes called the Persian Gulf. As I just said, Kuwait is a small country. Its land area is about 8,000 square miles, or in metric terms that's about 2,000,000 hectares. Kuwait's climate is one of the hottest in the world. It's one of the hottest. Let me give you an example of the range, of the difference, in temperatures in Kuwait. In the summer, the temperature often reaches 124° Fahrenheit during the day. That's about 51.1° on the Centigrade scale. Temperatures are naturally cooler during the winter. They range between 50° and 60° Fahrenheit during the day. In other words, they range between about 10° and 15.5° Celsius.

Did you manage to get down all the important information about Kuwait so far? Let's see. Kuwait's population is a little more than a million. It is located at the north end of the Arabian Gulf, or the Persian Gulf. Its land area is about 8,000 square miles or 2,000,000 hectares. Summer temperatures reach 124° Fahrenheit—they reach 51.1° Centigrade. Winter temperatures are between 50° and 60° Fahrenheit during the day, or between 10° and 15.5° Celsius. Check your notes. If you missed any of this information, you may want to rewind the tape and replay this section of the lecture. If you do have to rework this section of the lecture, try to increase your speed when taking notes.

Now back to the lecture.

Until oil was discovered there in 1938, Kuwait was a little-known country which was ruled by an Arab sheikh. Today this small desert country has become one of the world's leading oil producers; it has approximately 15 percent of the world's known petroleum reserves.

There wasn't as much information contained in this last bit of lecture as there was in the opening part of the lecture, was there? Did you write down that it was in 1938—in 1938—that oil was discovered, and that today it has about 15 percent of the world's known oil reserves? You're doing all right if you did manage to get down these facts. Let's go on.

Since the discovery of oil, Kuwait's rulers have turned the country into a prosperous welfare state. Kuwait has free primary and secondary education, free elementary and high school education, free health care and social services, and, believe it or not, Kuwaitis do not have to pay any personal income tax for those services. I might just add that in terms of national income per capita, Kuwait is one of the world's wealthiest nations. The per capita income was recently listed—in the late 1970s—as $11,431 per person. That's about 3,184 Dinars, as the Kuwaiti currency is called. As I mentioned before, Kuwait has free elementary and secondary education for its people. The rate of literacy is high in the country and is constantly growing. The University of Kuwait was opened in 1966, but many of the Kuwaiti students still study in colleges and universities abroad—at state expense, I might add.

All right. Did you note that Kuwait is a welfare state with free education, health care, and social services, and with no income tax? Did you also jot down that its per capita income is $11,431 or 3,184 Dinars per person per year. The University of Kuwait opened in 1966, but many students still study outside their country at government expense. O.K. Let's continue.

Now I would like to talk about the population of the country for a minute. Kuwait is, needless to point out, an Arab country, and about 99 percent of the people who live there are Moslems. That is, they follow the teachings of the prophet Mohammed. And yet, it is interesting to note that fewer than half of these Moslems are actually citizens of Kuwait. This is because there are many Moslem immigrants living and working there. Many of these recent immigrants have come from all over the Arab world—they've come from Egypt, Syria, Lebanon, from Oman, and from the Sudan. A lot of Indians, Pakistanis, and Iranians live and work in Kuwait, too. The other 1 percent of the population, in other words the non-Moslems, are recent immigrants who were attracted by the opportunities to work for the oil companies. There are several thousand Europeans and Americans in Kuwait. Many of them, as you might imagine, are employed by the oil companies.

Let me list the facts contained in this section of the lecture. Check your notes. 99 percent of the people are Moslems—half are citizens. The rest are from countries like Egypt, Syria, Lebanon, from Oman, the Sudan, from India, Pakistan, and

Iran. Some others—the non-Moslems—are from Europe and the U.S. Many work for the oil companies. Did you abbreviate the names of the countries the lecturer gave you? Can you look at your notes and identify the countries you listed with your abbreviations? I hope so. Let's continue.

Until the discovery of oil, most of the people in Kuwait lived in the traditional fashion, in the centuries-old fashion. Those who lived in the old, walled town of Kuwait lived in simple mud and brick houses. The people who lived outside the town were Bedouin nomads, and these Bedouins made their living raising camels, goats, and sheep. But today, almost all of the old, walled town is gone. It has been replaced by Kuwait City, the capital of the country. It's a modern urban center.

Check your notes. Before oil was discovered, people lived in the centuries-old fashion. Inside the city, there were simple mud houses. Outside were Bedouins raising camels, goats, and sheep. Today there is the modern Kuwait City. If this information had not been repeated for you, would you have been able to get it down in your notes? Soon you will have to learn to catch the information the first time it is given to you. Of course, if you were listening to a real lecture in a classroom, and you missed some of the information, you could raise your hand and ask the professor to repeat what he said. Now, let's finish taking notes about the country of Kuwait. Listen carefully.

It was only about twenty years ago, on June 19, 1961, that Kuwait gained its independence. Today, Kuwait, like England, is a constitutional monarchy whose head of state is the Emir. The Emir is chosen for life from the Sabah family by members of the family. That's spelled S–a–b–a–h, Sabah. This Sabah dynasty has ruled the country for over two hundred years. It was founded in 1756. Today, the Emir exercises executive power through a Prime Minister, a Council of fifteen members, and a National Assembly. This National Assembly's fifty members are elected by the citizens of Kuwait and serve for four-year terms. Naturally, only citizens of Kuwait are permitted to vote, that is, to participate in the country's politics, but all Kuwaiti residents—citizen or recent immigrant, Moslem or non-Moslem—do benefit from the country's free social services and from its wealth.

The lecture ended with a lot of information about the politics and government of Kuwait.   1. It gained independence on June 19, 1961.   2. It is a constitutional monarchy. The head of the state is the Emir—from the Sabah family.   3. The Sabah dynasty or family was founded in 1756.   4. There's a Prime Minister, a Council of fifteen members, and a National Assembly of fifty members—serving for four years; and last, only citizens vote, but all Kuwaitis benefit from the social services and wealth of the country.

Since much of the information was repeated or reiterated, you should have had quite enough time to take down all the facts. When you are tested on the information, you will have to do some calculations to answer the test questions. Are you ready for some tricky questions on the lecture information? Perhaps you should take a minute to compare your notes with those of the Note-Taking Model. Are they anything alike? There should be some similarities between your notes and the Model's. What similarities do you think I'm talking about?

Key to Preview of Vocabulary (Lecture 5)

1. dynasty
2. emir and sheikh
3. prosperous
4. Bedouin nomads
5. constitutional monarchy
6. per capita
7. reserves
8. income tax
9. executive power

Key to Multiple-Choice Questions (Lecture 5)

1. What is the difference in degrees Fahrenheit between the hottest temperature in the summer and the coldest temperature in the winter in Kuwait? (c)
2. What is the range in winter temperatures in Kuwait?   (b)
3. When was oil discovered in Kuwait?   (c)
4. What fraction of the world's known petroleum reserves does Kuwait have? (d)
5. According to the information given, how many dollars is 1 Dinar equal to? (b)
6. How many years after oil was discovered in Kuwait was the University of Kuwait opened?   (a)
7. What percentage of the people in Kuwait are not Moslem?   (a)
8. In the lecture, you heard mentioned some of the foreign countries that immigrants to Kuwait have come from. Which of the following countries was not mentioned in the lecture?   (d)
9. When did Kuwait become fully independent?   (d)
10. For how many years has the Sabah dynasty ruled Kuwait?   (b)
11. How many more members are there in the National Assembly than there are in the Emir's Council?   (b)

Key to True–False Statements (Lecture 5)

1. F   The Arabian Gulf is also sometimes called the Persian Gulf. The two names refer to the same body of water.
2. F   On the *Centigrade* scale, temperatures range between 15.5° and 10° on winter days.

3. T
4. F   Kuwaitis pay *no* personal income tax for social services.
5. T
6. T
7. T
8. F   Bedouin nomads used to live *outside* the old walled town.
9. T
10. F   The Emir of Kuwait is chosen by the members of the Sabah family.
11. T

LECTURE 6 MODEL

Languages in Conflict: Irish and English

The Republic of Ireland is a small country in northwestern Europe. It occupies most of the island of Ireland. Its land area is only 26,600 square miles. Its population is given at a little less than 3,000,000. A part of the island which is called Northern Ireland is a member of the British Commonwealth. Northern Ireland then is a political unit that is quite separate from the Republic of Ireland.

In the early Middle Ages—that is to say in the fifth and sixth centuries A.D.—Ireland was one of the principal cultural centers of Europe. You know, when the *barbarians* conquered the continent of Europe, it was Ireland that kept alive Western culture and learning. Later, however, in the twelfth century—that is to say in the late 1100s—the *Norman English* conquest of Ireland began. By the sixteenth century, England had gained control over the whole of Ireland. That is to say, by the 1500s England had subjugated the entire country. During this time, Irish lands were taken from their owners and given to the English and Scottish settlers. To be sure, the Irish people continually rebelled against the English, but these rebellions were always put down, or completely crushed. Throughout the eighteenth century—that is, throughout the 1700s—the Irish suffered from economic *exploitation* and political and religious *persecution*. As a result of this exploitation and persecution, the majority of the Irish people lived in great poverty.

In the late 1840s, a disaster hit Ireland; the potato crop failed because of the bad weather. You see, the potato had been the principal food of the majority of the Irish population up to that time. It is estimated that the population of Ireland in the 1830s was around 9 million people. In the four years after the potato crop failure, more than one million people died of *starvation*, and more than a million and a half people left Ireland in ships for Canada, the United States, and other countries. These ships were often called "floating *coffins*" because of the large number of people who died on board during the journey across the ocean.

In the early nineteenth century—in the early 1800s—Irish was spoken almost everywhere in Ireland. After the *Great Potato Famine* of 1847, however, and after the massive emigration of the following years, use of the Irish language in Ireland decreased rapidly. The English language replaced the Irish language. By 1870, only 20 percent of the Irish people spoke the national language. During the latter half of the nineteenth century—in other words from 1850 to 1900—English was the only language taught in the schools in Ireland, and English was the language of the politicians, the *clergy,* and the landlords. English was, in fact, the language of the rulers; while Irish, on the other hand, was the language of the ruled.

After years of struggle, Ireland finally achieved self-government from England in 1922 and became a free republic in 1949. At that time, nationalistic feelings of pride and independence from England started a movement in Ireland to make Irish the national language of Ireland. And so, the government *decreed* that knowledge of the Irish language was required for all elementary school teachers. As a result, by the year 1949, only 8.2 percent of the Irish teachers *lacked* a certificate to teach Irish to the school children. And today, Irish is a required subject in all state schools. Knowledge of Irish has been a requirement for college matriculation in Irish colleges since 1913 (except for the famous Trinity College in the capital city of Dublin). Today, all government papers issued must be in the two languages. Newspapers now publish articles in Irish as well as in English. And you can be sure that any Irish politician who wants to get elected in Ireland today must be able to make a speech in Irish, not just in English.

And so, the near-*extinction* of a language spoken for more than two thousand years has, perhaps, been slowed, or even stopped altogether.

LECTURE 6 NOTE-TAKING EXERCISE

The Republic of Ireland is a small country in northwestern Europe. It occupies most of the island of Ireland. Its land area is only 26,600 square miles. Its population is given at a little less than 3,000,000. A part of the island which is called Northern Ireland is a member of the British Commonwealth. Northern Ireland then is a political unit that is quite separate from the Republic of Ireland.

SCRIPT

All right, let's check your notes. The Republic of Ireland is in northwestern Europe. Its land area equals 26,600 square miles; its population a little less than 3,000,000. Northern Ireland is a member of the British Commonwealth and is politically separate from the Republic of Ireland, which is not a member of the Commonwealth.

Did you get down this information? Good. The next part of the lecture contains a good deal more information than this introductory part does. Get ready to take a lot of notes.

In the early Middle Ages—that is to say in the fifth and sixth centuries A.D.—Ireland was one of the principal cultural centers of Europe. That was in the fifth and sixth centuries. You know, when the barbarians conquered the continent of Europe, it was Ireland that kept alive Western culture and learning. Later, however, in the twelfth century— that is to say in the late 1100s—the Norman-English conquest of Ireland began. And by the sixteenth century, England had gained control over the whole of Ireland. That is to say, by the 1500s England had subjugated the entire country. During this time, Irish lands were taken from their owners and given to the English and Scottish settlers. To be sure, the Irish people continually rebelled against the English, but these rebellions were always put down, or completely crushed. Throughout the eighteenth century—that is, throughout the 1700s— the Irish suffered from economic exploitation and political and religious persecution. As a result of this exploitation and persecution, the majority of the Irish people lived in great poverty.

How did you do with your note-taking? Did you note: 1. In the fifth and sixth centuries Ireland was a principal cultural center. It managed to keep alive Western learning and culture when the barbarians overran Europe.   2. In the twelfth century—in the late 1100s—the Norman-English conquest began. By the sixteenth century England controlled Ireland. Irish lands were given to the English and Scottish settlers. Did you also get down that the Irish rebellions were put down and that the people suffered from economic exploitation and political and religious persecution? Because of this, the Irish people lived in awful poverty.
Did you manage to write down what you missed the first time? Good. Let's go on.

In the late 1840s a disaster hit Ireland; the potato crop failed because of the bad weather. You see, the potato had been the principal food of the majority of the Irish population at that time. It is estimated that the population of Ireland in the 1830s was around 9 million people. In the four years after the potato crop failure, more than one million people died of starvation, and more than a million and a half people left Ireland in ships for Canada, the United States, and other countries. These ships were often called "floating coffins" because of the large number of people who died on board during the journey across the ocean.

O.K. There were several important dates and figures in this section of the lecture. Did you get them down? Check your notes. In the late 1840s the potato crop failed because of bad weather. The potato had been the principal food—the staple—of the people. The Irish population had been around 9 million in the 1830s. After the crop failure, one million died and a million and a half left in "floating coffins" for Canada, the U.S.A, and other countries. So many died during the ocean journey. How are you doing with your note-taking? Fine, I hope. Let's continue with the lecture.

In the early nineteenth century—in the early 1800s—Irish was spoken almost everywhere in Ireland. After the Great Potato Famine of 1847, however, and after the massive emigration of the following years, the use of the Irish national language decreased rapidly. The English language replaced the Irish language. By 1870, only 20 percent of the Irish people spoke the national language. During the latter half of the nineteenth century—in other words from 1850 to 1900—English was the only language taught in the schools in Ireland, and English was the language of the politicians, the clergy, and the landlords. English was, in fact, the language of the rulers, while Irish was the language of the ruled.

O.K. Let's go over the facts. In the early 1800s Irish was spoken almost everywhere in Ireland. After the Potato Famine of 1847 and the massive emigration from Ireland, use of Irish decreased. It was replaced by the English language. By 1870 only 20 percent of the people spoke Irish. From 1850 to 1900, English was the only language taught in the schools, and it was the politicians', the clergy's, and the landlords' language. It was the rulers' language. All right. Let's continue. This time, however, the information contained in this part of the lecture will not be repeated for you. So you must catch the facts and write them down as soon as you hear them. Are you ready?

After years of struggle, Ireland finally achieved self-government from England in 1922 and became a free republic in 1949. At that time, nationalistic feelings of pride and independence from England started a movement in Ireland to make Irish the national language of Ireland. And so, the government decreed that knowledge of the Irish language was required for all elementary school teachers. As a result, by the year 1949, only 8.2 percent of all the Irish teachers lacked a certificate to teach Irish to the school children. And today, Irish is a required subject in all state schools. Knowledge of Irish has been a requirement for college matriculation in Irish colleges since 1913 (except for the famous Trinity College in the capital city of Dublin). Today, all government papers issued must be in the two languages. Newspapers now publish articles in Irish as well as in English. And you can be sure that any Irish politician who wants to get elected in Ireland today must be able to make a speech in Irish, not just in English.

And so, the near-extinction of a language spoken for more than two thousand years has, perhaps, been slowed down, or even stopped altogether.

This is the first time that lecture details have not been repeated for you to make sure that you could write them down. How did you do? Well, we shall see when you answer the questions on this last part of the lecture. Remember, less and less of the lecture will be repeated for you as we continue working through these note-taking exercises.

All right, let's begin the quiz on the lecture information. Have your notes ready to help answer the questions.

Key to Preview of Vocabulary (Lecture 6)

1. barbarians
2. exploitation
3. Norman-English
4. clergy
5. coffin
6. persecution
7. Great Potato Famine
8. extinction
9. lack
10. decree
11. starvation

Key to Multiple-Choice Questions (Lecture 6)

1. What is the current population of Ireland?   (c)
2. When was Ireland one of the principal cultural centers of Europe?   (c)
3. When did England gain control over the whole of Ireland?   (d)
4. What did the Irish people experience throughout the eighteenth century? (d)
5. When the potato crop failed, what happened in Ireland?   (a)
6. In exactly what year did the Great Potato Famine occur?   (c)
7. When was it that English was the only language taught in Ireland's schools?   (d)
8. When did Ireland achieve self-government?   (a)
9. When did Ireland become a republic?   (d)
10. In the 1940s which group was required to know Irish?   (b)
11. Since what year has Irish been required for college matriculation in every college in Ireland except in Trinity College?   (b)
12. How long has the Irish language been spoken in Ireland?   (d)

Key to True–False Statements (Lecture 6)

1. T
2. T
3. F   The Irish continually *rebelled* against the English down through the ages.
4. F   The Irish suffered from economic exploitation, *and* religious and political persecution.
5. F   The failure of the potato crop brought starvation to those who remained in Ireland.
6. T
7. T
8. T
9. F   The government prints all its documents in *both* English and Irish.
10. F   Newspaper articles are printed in both English and Irish today.
11. F   It has been spoken in Ireland for over a thousand years—it has been spoken in one form or another for more than *two* thousand years.

LECTURE 7 MODEL

Women's Liberation: The Search for Equality

The Women's Liberation movement has become an important social movement throughout much of the world today. In the past few decades, it has become one of the most important social movements in the U.S. Women have been fighting for equal rights in the United States since the early 1900s, but it was really in the 1960s and '70s that women began to gain equal rights and treatment in the fields of politics, education, employment, and the home.

SCRIPT

As for the field of politics, today's politicians are well aware that women have become a powerful political force in this country. One of the reasons for this is that there are about 70 million women of voting age. (Voting age in the United States, as many of you may already know, is eighteen.) There are, in fact, 7 million more women of voting age than there are men of voting age in the U.S. today.

Not only are there more women voting these days and influencing the political structure of the country, but more of them are becoming better educated. Today's young American woman is much more likely to be a college student than her mother was. In 1950, only 7 percent of all women eighteen to twenty-four years old were enrolled in college. By 1980, 30 percent of all women in this age group were college students. Today in the United States, there are at least 5 million women college graduates. To be sure, this is 2.3 million fewer than the number of

American men with college degrees, but the number is growing each year.

As far as the field of employment is concerned, about 42 percent of the entire American work force today is made up of women; there are 38.8 million women workers. In contrast, back in 1900, only 20 percent of the country's work force was made up of women. This seems to indicate that greater numbers of today's women are managing to combine careers outside the home with the traditional *roles* of wife, mother, and homemaker. Years ago, you see, it was customary for women to work outside the home only until they got married or until they had children. Nowadays, many women are continuing to work after they marry, and even after they have children.

Now what brought about this increase in the number of women working outside the home? Well, it all began with World War II. During the war, large numbers of women began to enter the job market. Many took the jobs of the men who were *drafted* into military service. A great many of these women became factory workers, and they proved themselves to be *capable* and *dependable* workers. Just recently, by the way, I read that a factory manager in Japan stated that the introduction of women workers on two factory assembly lines resulted in a productivity increase of 10 percent and a labor cost decrease of 15 percent. As I said earlier, women proved to be capable and dependable workers during the war, so after the war, many of them were asked to remain at their jobs.

Although there are so many women in the labor force today, they are still facing many problems. For one thing, women workers do not yet receive equal treatment in the job market, either in the area of *hiring,* or in the area of *salary.* Let me explain what I mean by this. In 1980, the mean, or the average, salary for a college-educated man was $15,446.00 per year, while the mean income for a college-educated woman was only $8,633.00 per year. This means that the average income for an American man was about 56 percent higher than it was for an American woman. Perhaps I should cite that one of the reasons given for the *disparity* in pay is that most women in the U.S. work in low-paying jobs. Approximately 33 1/3 percent of all employed women today are still working as bookkeepers, secretaries, and clerks. They receive very low pay for their work. Only 16 percent of all women workers are professional or technical workers, such as doctors, teachers, and scientists. Professionals, naturally, receive higher salaries for their work. Another reason for the disparity in pay is that women often quit their jobs to have babies, and they lose their seniority when they do so, as a result. And yet, today women can be found working in fields that were closed to them years ago. They are now working as corporate executives, officers in the armed forces, as politicians, lawyers, and even as construction workers, *plumbers,* policewomen, and, yes, even as astronauts.

Today, women are no longer willing to accept the idea of being *second-class citizens* in school, at work, in their marriages, or in their homes. They are often demanding that their husbands help with the housework and with the raising of children. Nowadays, women are becoming better educated. They are increasing their job opportunities and their earning power. They are participating in politics more. Yes, they are enjoying new freedoms, new opportunities, new responsibilities, and, I might add, new headaches.

LECTURE 7 NOTE-TAKING EXERCISE

In the last few decades, the Women's Liberation Movement has become one of the most important social movements in the United States. In the past few decades, it has become an important social movement throughout the rest of the world, too. Women have been fighting for equal rights in the U.S. since the early 1900s, but it was in the 1960s and '70s that women really began to gain equal rights and treatment in the fields of politics, education, employment, and the home. As for the field of politics, today's politicians are quite aware that women have become a powerful political force in this country. In the United States there are about 70 million women of voting age. (Voting age in the United States, as many of you may already know, is eighteen.) There are, in fact, 7 million more women of voting age than there are men of voting age in the U.S. today.

SCRIPT

How are you doing with getting down the important information? I'll ask a few questions about the important facts. Look at the notes you've taken so far. Can you answer these questions? If you can, then you did get down the most important information in this part of the lecture. 1. When was it that women really began to gain equal rights in politics, education, employment, and the home? Did you write down in your notes that it was in the 1960s and '70s? Good. Did you also abbreviate the list of fields I just mentioned? 2. How many women are there of voting age in the United States? What is the voting age in the U.S.? And finally, how many more women of voting age than men are there in the U.S.? Well, if you could find the answers to each of these questions by checking the notes you just took, you are doing just fine. If you could not answer the questions, or if you did not have time to jot down the facts, you may want to go back and listen to this part of the lecture again and practice speeding up your note-taking. O.K., let's go on now.

Not only are there more women voting these days, but more of them are becoming better educated. Today's young woman is much more likely to be a college student than her mother was. In 1950, only 7 percent of all women eighteen to twenty-four years old were in college. By 1980, 30 percent of all women in this age group were enrolled in college. Today in the United States, there are at least 5 million women college graduates. To be sure, this is 2.3 million fewer than the number of American men with college degrees, but the number of women college graduates is growing each year.

Take a moment's break to catch your breath. There were quite a few statistics given in this part of the lecture. Did you write each one down? They will not be repeated for you here. This is so that you can practice taking down information at the same time you're hearing it. Let's continue with the lecture.

As far as the field of employment is concerned, about 42 percent of the entire American work force today is made up of women—approximately 42 percent. There are 38.8 million women workers. In contrast, back in 1900, only 20 percent of the country's work force was made up of women. This seems to indicate that greater numbers of today's women are managing to combine careers outside the home with the traditional roles of wife, of mother, and of homemaker. They are combining careers with their traditional roles of wife, mother, and homemaker. Years ago, you see, it was customary for women to work only until they got married or until they had children. That's until they married or until they had children. Nowadays, many women are continuing to work after they marry, and even after they have children.

Are you keeping up with the lecturer? Good.

Now, what brought about this increase in the number of women working outside the home? Well, it all began with World War II. During the war, large numbers of women first began to enter the job market. They began to enter the labor force. Many took the jobs of the men who were drafted for military service. A great many of these women became factory workers, and they proved themselves to be capable and dependable workers. They were quite capable and dependable.

Just recently, by the way, I read that a factory manager in Japan stated that the introduction of women workers on two factory assembly lines resulted in a productivity increase of 10 percent and a labor cost decrease of 15 percent. Let me repeat those figures— employing women led to a productivity increase of 10 percent and a labor cost decrease or reduction of 15 percent. As I said earlier, women proved to be capable and dependable workers during the war, so after the war, many of them were asked to remain at their jobs.

Did you get all that down? Let's check that you did. I'll list the important facts in this last segment for you again. World War II resulted in the influx of women into the job market—to take the place of the men who were drafted. Did you indicate that many women became factory workers and that they were capable and dependable? Maybe you listed only one of these words— capable or dependable. They mean nearly the same thing, so one of them would have been sufficient. You could also have put down into your notes that they were good workers. Right? Did you get down that women brought about a 10 percent increase in productivity and a 15 percent decrease in cost for the Japanese factory manager? Great. Let's go on.

Although there are so many women in the labor force today, they are still facing many problems. For one thing, women workers do not yet receive equal treatment in the job market, either in the area of hiring, or in the area of salary—in hiring or in salary. Let me explain what I mean by this. In 1980 the mean, or the average, salary for a college-educated man was $15,446.00 per year, while the mean income for a college-educated woman was only $8,633.00 per year. This means that the average income for an American man was about 56 percent higher than it was for an American woman. Perhaps I should cite that one of the reasons given for this disparity—for the difference—in pay is that most women in the U.S. work in low-paying jobs. Approximately 33 1/3 percent of all employed women today are still working as bookkeepers, secretaries, and clerks. They receive very low pay for their work. Only 16 percent of all women workers are professional or technical workers, such as doctors, teachers, and scientists. Professionals, naturally, receive higher salaries for their work. Another reason for this disparity in pay is that women often quit their jobs to have babies, and they lose their seniority when they do so. And yet, today women can be found working in fields that were closed to them years ago. They are now working as corporate executives, officers in the armed forces, as politicians, as lawyers, and even as construction workers, as plumbers, policewomen, and, yes, even as astronauts.

Today, women are no longer willing to accept the idea of being second-class citizens in school, at work, in their marriages, or in their homes. They are demanding that their husbands help with the housework and with the raising of the children. They aren't always getting what they demand, but... Nowadays, women are becoming better educated. They are increasing their job opportunities and their earning power. They are participating in politics more. Yes, they are enjoying new freedoms, new opportunities, new responsibilities, and, I might add, new headaches.

Well now, are you exhausted? I'll bet. How did you do with the note-taking? Why don't you take a minute to compare your notes with those of the model. Fill in any gaps you have in your notes. When you've done that, get ready to take the test covering the information.

Key to Preview of Vocabulary (Lecture 7)

1. role
2. capable
3. drafted/drafted
4. dependable
5. plumber
6. disparity
7. second-class citizen
8. salary
9. hiring

Key to Multiple-Choice Questions (Lecture 7)

1. Number one is a bit tricky. Listen carefully. About how many *men* of voting age are there in the United States? (c)
2. What percent of all women eighteen to twenty-four years old were enrolled in college in 1950? (a)
3. How much greater a percentage of women were enrolled in college in 1980 than in 1950? (d)
4. How many women college graduates are there in the United States today? (b)
5. How many men college graduates are there in the United States today? (c)
6. What percent of the labor force of 1900 was made up of women? (b)
7. What happened when Japanese women workers were introduced on two assembly lines? (b)
8. What was the average annual salary of a college-educated woman in 1980? (b)
9. What was the average annual salary of a college-educated man in 1980? (c)
10. What percent of women today work as bookkeepers, secretaries, and clerks? (b)
11. What percent of women workers are professionals or technical workers? (b)

Key to True–False Statements (Lecture 7)

1. T
2. T
3. T
4. F   *Fifty-eight percent* of the work force is made up of men.
5. F   It was customary for women to work *until* they had children.
6. F   The influx is attributed to the start of *World War II.*

7. T
8. F   She earns $.56 for every dollar a man makes.
9. T
10. T
11. F   She says that they have new freedoms, new opportunities, and new *headaches*. The problems are different, but they are still there.

LECTURE 8 MODEL

The Panama Canal: A Great Engineering Achievement

I'll start off my talk with a few simple statements of facts: the Panama Canal connects the Atlantic Ocean and the Pacific Ocean. It is located at the narrowest part of Panama, which is, of course, the Central American country that connects North and South America. Let me also say that the *fame* of the Panama Canal is not in its size. It's not a big canal at all. In fact, it's only 50.72 miles long. In metric measurement that's about 81.65 kilometers long. In comparison, the Suez Canal in Egypt is 103 miles or about 166 kilometers long. And yet, even though the Panama Canal is not very large, it is still considered to be one of the greatest engineering achievements. When it was first built it had a tremendous impact on East–West trade. It brought the Orient and the West closer together. What it actually did was it brought the Atlantic and Pacific coastlines of the United States closer together. Let me explain what I mean by this by giving an example. Before the Canal existed, a ship that was sailing from New York to San Francisco had to travel more than 13,000 miles or, let's say, 20,930 kilometers around the tip of South America. The Canal shortened this trip to about 5,200 miles—that meant that a ship had to travel about 8,370 kilometers from New York to San Francisco.

Now let me say a few words about the history of the Canal. There had long been a great deal of interest in the development of a canal in the Panama region when the United States began to build the Canal. For many years the early Spaniards had unsuccessfully searched for a natural waterway that joined the Atlantic and Pacific Oceans. You see, these early Spaniards needed a more efficient way to ship the treasures of the *Inca Empire* and their other South American colonies back to Spain. That is to say, to ship the stolen gold and silver by water would have been much easier and more efficient than to ship it over land. And so, as early as 1534, King Charles I of Spain ordered a *survey* of the area to determine whether it was possible to construct a canal in the area for "greater efficiency." Reports, however, indicated that it was completely impossible to construct a sea-level—a *sea-level*—canal there at that time. They just didn't have the machinery or the technology to do the job back then.

It was more than 300 years later, in 1882, when a French company actually began construction of a canal in the Panama region. The engineer who built the Suez Canal, Ferdinand de Lesseps, directed the construction of the Canal; however, disease, and what some have called mismanagement forced the French company *to abandon the undertaking*. In June of 1902, the U.S. bought the French company's *concession*. The United States paid the Panamanian government $10 million, and it began constructing the Panama Canal. The 1903 treaty with Panama gave the U.S. the right to build and operate the Canal and to govern the Canal Zone. (The Canal Zone is a strip of land that extends for five miles on either side of the Canal. In other words, it extends eight kilometers on either side of the Canal.)

In building the Canal, thousands of workers labored for many years under the supervision of Dr. William Gorgas and Colonel George Goethals. Hospital records of the time show that 5,609 workers died as a result of disease and accidents during the U.S. construction work. All in all, construction of the Panama Canal cost the U.S. $380 million. I might add that this was certainly a very profitable investment for the United States because recent figures show that the Panama Canal Company collected $134 million in *tolls* on the Canal in one year alone.

As for the actual working of the Panama Canal, it has three sets of water-filled chambers or, what are more commonly called *locks*. These locks raise and lower the ships from one level to another. (The Panama Canal is not a sea-level canal, by the way.) The locks were built in pairs so that ships could pass through in both directions at the same time. Passage through the locks takes approximately seven to eight hours. Each of the locks has a usable length of 1,000 feet or 300 meters. Each has a width of 110 feet or 33 meters, and each has a depth of about seventy feet—that's a depth of about twenty-one meters. As I said previously, the Canal is small. The dimensions of the locks do limit the size of ships that can use it. There's little doubt that by the year 2000, the present Canal will be unable to service the world's shipping needs. This is because larger and larger ships are being built. Certainly larger locks will be required to accommodate these newer, larger ships.

Before I finish up, I'll say a word or two about the *dispute* that arose in the 1960s concerning the control of both the Canal and the Canal Zone. The government of Panama wanted to control and operate the Panama Canal and to govern the Canal Zone. The U.S. had done so since it was first opened. In the late 1970s a treaty was drawn up to resolve this dispute. The treaty provided for Panama to gain full control of the *strategic* waterway by the year 2000. Panama will then own, manage, and operate one of the greatest engineering achievements.

LECTURE 8 NOTE-TAKING EXERCISE

The Panama Canal: A Great Engineering Achievement

I'll start off my talk with a few simple statements of facts: the Panama Canal connects the Atlantic Ocean and the Pacific Ocean. The Canal is located at the narrowest part of Panama, which is, of course, the Central American country that connects North and South America. Let me also say that the fame of the Panama Canal is not in its size. It's not famous for its size. It's not a big canal at all. In fact, it's only 50.72 miles long. In metric measurement that's 81.65 kilometers long. Just in comparison, let me point out that the Suez Canal in Egypt is 103 miles long or about 166 kilometers long. And yet, even though the Panama Canal is not very large, it is still considered to be a great engineering achievement, one of our very greatest achievements, and when it was first built it had a tremendous impact on East-West trade. It brought the Orient and the West closer together. What it actually did was it brought the Atlantic and Pacific coastlines of the United States closer together. Let me explain what I mean by this by giving an example. Before the Canal existed, a ship that was sailing from New York to San Francisco had to travel more than 13,000 miles or, let's say 20,930 kilometers, around the tip of South America. The Canal shortened this trip to about 5,200 miles— that meant that a ship had to travel about 8,370 kilometers from New York to San Francisco.

O.K. How are you doing so far? Take a look at your notes for a minute. Did you miss any of the information? If you did, why don't you rewind the tape and listen to that part of the lecture again. Fill in the gaps in your notes as you listen for the second time. If you did manage to get all the information down, take a moment to see if you can reconstruct your notes into a short talk on the Panama Canal's location, size, and importance. Turn off the tape while you reconstruct the lecture from your notes.

O.K. Now let's get back to taking some more notes.

Now let me say a few words about the history of the Canal. There had long been a great deal of interest in the development of a canal in the Panama region when the United States began to build the Canal. For many years the early Spaniards had unsuccessfully searched for a natural waterway that joined the Atlantic and Pacific Oceans. You see, these early Spaniards needed a more efficient way to ship the treasures of the Inca Empire and their other South American colonies back to Spain. That is to say, to ship the stolen gold and silver by water would have been much easier and more efficient than to ship it over land. And so, as early as 1534, King Charles I of Spain ordered a survey of the area to determine whether it was possible to construct a canal in the area for "greater efficiency." Reports, however, indicated that it was completely impossible to construct a sea-level, I said—a *sea-level,*—canal there at that time. They just didn't have the machinery or the technology to do the job back then.

It was more than 300 years later, in 1882, when a French company actually began construction of a canal in the Panama region. The engineer who built the Suez Canal, Ferdinand de Lesseps, directed the construction of the Canal; de Lesseps is spelled d–e L–e–s–s–e–p–s. However, disease, and what some have called mismanagement forced the French company to abandon the undertaking—to stop work on the project. In June of 1902, the United States bought the French company's concession. The U.S. paid the Panamanian government $10 million, and it began constructing the Panama Canal. The 1903 treaty with Panama gave the U.S. the right to build and to operate the Canal and to govern the Canal Zone. (The Canal Zone is a strip of land that extends for five miles on either side of the Canal. In other words, it extends eight kilometers on either side of the Canal.)

In building the Canal, thousands of workers worked for many years under the supervision of Dr. William Gorgas and Colonel George Goethals. Hospital records of the time show that 5,609 workers died as a result of disease and accidents during the U.S. construction work. All in all, construction of the Panama Canal cost the U.S. $380 million. I might add that this was certainly a very profitable investment for the United States because recent figures show that the Panama Canal Company collected $134 million in tolls on the Canal in one year alone.

All right. Hold it for a minute. Are you keeping up with the lecturer? Are you getting the facts down? Think about the topic of that last part of the lecture. What was the topic of that section? Was it the size, location, importance, or history of the Canal? It was the history. There were several dates given. Did you get them down? Look at your notes and see if you can find the answers for the following questions: Why did the early Spaniards want a canal in the Panama region? Why was it impossible to build a sea-level canal in Panama in the 1500s? Why did the French company stop work on building the Panama Canal? Why was building the Canal a profitable investment for the U.S.? Why did so many workers die during the U.S. construction of the Canal? Let's go back to the lecture.

As for the actual working of the Panama Canal, it has three sets of water-filled chambers or, what are more commonly called, locks. These locks raise and lower ships from one level to another. (The Panama Canal is not a sea-level canal, by the way.) The locks were built in pairs so that ships could pass through in both directions at the same time. Passage through the locks takes approximately seven to eight hours. Each of the locks has a usable length of 1,000 feet or 300 meters. Each has a width of 110 feet or 39 meters, and each lock has a depth of about 70 feet—that's a depth of about 21 meters. As I said previously, the Canal is small. The dimensions of the locks do limit the size of the ships that can use it. There's little doubt that by the year 2000, the present Canal will be unable to service the world's shipping needs. This is because larger and larger ships are being built. Certainly larger locks will be required to accommodate these newer, larger ships.

Before I finish up, I'll say a word or two about the dispute that arose in the 1960s concerning the control of both the Canal and the Canal Zone. The government of Panama wanted to control and operate the Panama Canal and to govern the Canal Zone. The U.S. had done so since it was first opened. In the late 1970s a treaty was drawn up to resolve this dispute. The treaty provided for Panama to gain full control of the strategic waterway by the year 2000. Panama will then own, manage, and operate one of the greatest engineering achievements.

Well, did you maintain a good pace taking your notes? What two topics did the lecturer take up during this part of the lecture? Right. They were the actual working of the Canal—the length, width, and depth of the locks—and the smallness of the locks. And he finally talked about the dispute over the control of the Canal. Look over your notes and see if they need any fixing up before we go on to the testing section.

Key to Preview of Vocabulary (Lecture 8)

1. toll
2. fame
3. survey
4. lock
5. to abandon the undertaking
6. concession
7. Inca Empire
8. dispute
9. strategic

Key to Multiple-Choice Questions (Lecture 8)

1. How many miles long is the Panama Canal?   (a)
2. Before the Canal existed, how many kilometers did a ship going from New York to San Francisco have to travel?   (d)
3. By how many miles did the Canal shorten the trip from New York to San Francisco?   (b)
4. Why did the early Spaniards want a canal in the Panama region?   (a)
5. How many years after King Charles I ordered his survey was construction of a canal in Panama begun?   (c)

6. Why did the French company abandon the construction of a canal in Panama?   (d)
7. How much did the United States government pay the Panamanian government in 1902?   (b)
8. How much did construction of the canal cost the U.S.?   (d)
9. What is the difference in the amount of money it cost the U.S. to build the Canal and the amount of money the United States received in tolls in one year alone?   (c)
10. How long is each Canal lock?   (b)
11. How wide is each Canal lock?   (a)
12. How deep is each Canal lock?   (a)

Key to True–False Statements (Lecture 8)

1. T
2. F   The Suez Canal is *longer* than the Panama Canal.
3. T
4. T
5. F   They indicated *pessimism* about the possibility.
6. T
7. T
8. T
9. F   Thousands of workers died during construction. This must have disrupted the work.
10. F   The Canal was a profitable investment for the U.S. Notice the amount of revenue that is received in one year in tolls.
11. T
12. F   Each lock is seventy feet deep or twenty-one meters deep.
13. F   The larger ships will not be able to pass through, but smaller ships should still be able to sail through.
14. F   By the year 2000, Panama will be in full control.

LECTURE 9 MODEL

T. E. Lawrence: Lawrence of Arabia

You might say that Thomas Edward Lawrence, or as he is more often called, Lawrence of Arabia, was one of the most adventurous, colorful European personalities to come out of World War I. But before I talk about the role he played in World War I, let me first say a word or two about his background—about his boyhood and youth. He was born on August 15, 1888, in Wales. He spent his early childhood in France, but most of his boyhood and youth in Oxford, England. When he was in college, he became keenly interested in *archaeology,* especially in Middle Eastern archaeology. While he was in college, he also studied Arabic, so he had actually gained some knowledge of the language and culture of the Middle East long before the war began. His knowledge of Arabic would prove of great benefit to him during the war.

When World War I broke out in 1914, Lawrence was assigned to the *intelligence section* of the British army. At that time, Britain was at war with Germany and Turkey. The British leaders desperately wanted an Arab rebellion against the Turks to erupt—to begin—and, of course, to succeed in order to secure victory for England against the Turks. As you may know, in the early 1900s the *Ottoman Empire* controlled virtually the whole of the Arabian peninsula. However, secret Arab societies, such as the Ahab and the Fetah, were busy preparing a rebellion—an uprising—against the Turks. One of the leaders of this planned rebellion was a man called Feisal al Hussein, who became a friend and comrade of Lawrence. And so, this young Arabic-speaking Englishman, T. E. Lawrence, was sent by the British government to Arabia to help organize the Arab revolt against the Turks from 1916 to 1918. He joined the Arab forces under Feisal al Hussein (Feisal I). Now in order to *weld* the *scattered* Arab forces into a fighting unit, the Englishman adopted an Arab lifestyle: he spoke only Arabic, wore Arab clothing, and rode a camel rather than a horse. You might say he followed the rule: "When in Rome, do as the Romans do." While fighting alongside the Arabs, it appears that he became passionately devoted to the cause of Arab liberation and independence; moreover, he promised his Arab friends to work for their liberation from colonial rule. Lawrence and his Arab comrades used *guerilla-type* tactics, instead of conventional-type warfare, with the result that a few thousand Arab guerillas succeeded in tying down and in crippling the Turkish forces. One of the most daring and important things they did was the sabotaging of the supply trains in *Hejaz*. Well, this eventually led to the defeat of the Turks and to victory for both the Arabs and the *Allies*.

After World War I ended, Lawrence went with the British delegation to the Paris Peace Conference of 1919. It was, to be exact, in January of 1919 that he went. At the conference, he unsuccessfully pleaded for Arabian independence. What he did actually was this: he promoted the formation of independent Arab states. Remember, during the war, he had promised freedom to the Arabs in the name of Great Britain. The Arabs certainly would not have fought against the Turks just to pass from Turkish hands into those of the English and the French. And yet, this is exactly what happened after the war! Lawrence was not able to make his country keep the promise he had made in its name.

From 1921 to 1922, Lawrence served as adviser on Arab affairs in the Middle East Division of the Colonial Office, but he became so deeply disappointed and so very frustrated by postwar British policy toward the Arabs that he resigned from the Colonial Office. He seems to have felt that his failure to win Arab independence had betrayed his Arab friends. On August 30, 1922, he enlisted in the Royal Air Force and later in March of 1923 in the British *tank corps*. Both times he enlisted under *pseudonyms*—under false names. Instead of the fame and glory war heroes usually seek and receive, he sought *seclusion* and *anonymity*. During this time of seclusion, he wrote several books. One of them, *The Seven Pillars of Wisdom,* is the story of his experiences in Arabia.

It seems *ironic,* indeed, that after all the dangers Lawrence had faced and all the battles he had fought during the war, his life should come to an end not on the desert field of battle but on a peaceful English country road in May of 1935. He was killed in a motorcycle accident.

Let me finish up by saying a word or two about how people react to this colorful Englishman. He has been called a hero by some and a traitor by others. To some, he is a saint. To others, a devil. His admirers consider him a courageous, dedicated leader of men. His critics consider him an ambitious, weak, confused man. Whatever people may think, Lawrence of Arabia, to be sure, was an unusual, strange, and complex Englishman, a *living legend* of the early 1900s.

LECTURE 9 NOTE-TAKING EXERCISE

T. E. Lawrence: Lawrence of Arabia

SCRIPT

You might say that Thomas Edward Lawrence, or as he is more often called, Lawrence of Arabia, was one of the most adventurous, colorful European personalities to come out of World War I. But before I talk about the role he played in World War I, let me first say a word or two about his background—about his boyhood and youth. He was born on August 15, 1888 in Wales. He spent his early childhood in France, but most of his boyhood and youth in Oxford, England. Let me spell Wales for you. It's spelled W–a–l–e–s. Got it? O.K. When he was in college, Lawrence became keenly interested in archaeology. He became especially interested in Middle Eastern archaeology—in the archaeology of the Middle East. While he was in college, he also studied Arabic, so he had actually gained some knowledge of the language and culture of the Middle East long before the war began. His knowledge of Arabic would prove—would be—of great benefit to him during the war.

When World War I broke out in 1914—when it began in 1914—Lawrence was assigned to the intelligence section of the British army. At that time, Britain was at war with Germany and Turkey. The British leaders desperately wanted an Arab rebellion against the Turks to erupt—to begin—and, of course, to succeed in order to secure victory for England against the Turks. As you may know, in the early 1900s the Ottoman Empire controlled virtually the whole of the Arabian peninsula; I said the Ottoman Empire virtually controlled Arabia. However, secret Arab societies, such as the Ahab and the Fetah, were busy preparing a rebellion against the Turks. That's the Ahab (spelled A–h–a–b) and the Fetah (spelled F–e–t–a–h). One of the leaders of this planned rebellion was a man called Feisal al Hussein. Let me repeat that name for you. That's Feisal al Hussein. He became a friend and comrade of Lawrence. As I said earlier, Lawrence was sent by the British government to Arabia to help organize the Arab revolt against the Turks from 1916 to 1918. He joined the Arab forces under Feisal al Hussein, who is called also Feisal the First. Now, in order to weld the scattered Arab forces into a fighting unit, Lawrence adopted an Arab lifestyle. In other words, he spoke only Arabic; he wore Arab clothing; and he rode on camels rather than on horses. You might say he followed the rule: "When in Rome, do as the Romans do." While fighting alongside the Arabs, it appears that he became devoted—even passionately devoted—to the cause of Arab liberation and independence; moreover, he promised his Arab friends to work for their liberation from colonial rule. Lawrence and his Arab comrades used guerilla-type tactics instead of conventional-type warfare, with the result that a few thousand Arab guerillas succeeded in tying down and in crippling—in actually destroying—the Turkish forces. One of the most daring things they did was the sabotaging of the supply trains in Hejaz. Well, all this eventually led to the defeat of the Turks and to victory for both the Arabs and the Allies.

After World War I ended, Lawrence went with the British delegation to the Paris Peace Conference of 1919. He went with the British delegation to the 1919 Paris Peace Conference. At the conference, he unsuccessfully pleaded for Arab independence. What he actually did was this: he promoted the formation of independent Arab states. Remember, during the war, he had promised freedom to the Arabs in the name of Great Britain. The Arabs certainly would not have rebelled and fought against the Turks just to pass from Turkish hands into those of the English and French. And yet, this is exactly what happened after the war. This is exactly what happened! Lawrence was not able to make his country keep the promise he had made in its name.

From 1921 to 1922, Lawrence served as adviser on Arab affairs in the Middle East Division of the Colonial Office. That's from 1921 to 1922. But he became so deeply disappointed and so very frustrated by postwar British policy toward the Arabs that he resigned from the Colonial Office. He seems to have felt that his failure to win Arab independence had betrayed his Arab friends. On August 30, 1922, he enlisted in the Royal Air Force and later in March of 1923 in the British tank corps, both times under pseudonyms—under false names. Instead of the fame and glory war heroes usually receive, he sought seclusion and anonymity. During this time of seclusion, he wrote several books. One of them, *The Seven Pillars of Wisdom,* is the story of his experiences in Arabia.

It seems ironic indeed that, after all the dangers Lawrence had faced and all the battles he had fought during the war, his life should come to an end not on the desert field of battle but on a peaceful English country road in May of 1935. He was killed in a motorcycle accident.

O.K. Let me finish up by saying a word or two about how people react to this colorful Englishman. He has been called a hero by some and a traitor by others. To some he is a saint. To others, a devil. His admirers consider him a courageous, dedicated leader of men. His critics consider him a weak and confused man. Whatever people may think, Lawrence of Arabia was, to be sure, an unusual, strange, and complex Englishman, a living legend of the early 1900s.

Key to Preview of Vocabulary (Lecture 9)

1. guerilla-type tactics
2. Hejaz
3. archaeology
4. pseudonym
5. intelligence section
6. a living legend
7. to weld
8. scattered
9. Allies
10. tank corps
11. Ottoman Empire
12. seclusion
13. anonymity
14. ironic

Key to Multiple-Choice Questions (Lecture 9)

1. When was T. E. Lawrence born?   (a)
2. When did Lawrence help organize the Arab revolt against the Ottoman Empire?   (b)
3. What did Lawrence and the Arab guerillas sabotage in Hejaz?   (c)
4. After World War I, with what delegation did Lawrence go to the Paris Peace Conference?   (b)
5. From 1921 to 1922 where did Lawrence serve as an adviser on Arab affairs?   (c)
6. What did Lawrence do after he resigned from the Colonial Office?   (d)
7. When did Lawrence enlist in the tank corps?   (c)
8. What is *The Seven Pillars of Wisdom* primarily the story of?   (b)
9. How old was Lawrence when he was killed in a motorcycle accident?   (b)
10. How did Lawrence's critics describe him?   (b)

Key to True–False Statements (Lecture 9)

1. ?   We are told where he spent his childhood, but nothing about whether it was a happy or unhappy one.
2. F   He first studied Arabic when he was in college in *England*.

3. T   Wales; France; England.

4. T

5. T

6. ?   Very little is said about Feisal, and nothing is said about what he did after the war.

7. T

8. F   He was *not* able to do so.

9. T

10. T

11. ?   We are told nothing about Lawrence's co-workers in the Colonial Office.

12. F   He was a deeply disappointed and frustrated man.

13. F   He sought *seclusion* and *anonymity* after the war.

14. ?   We are told that he had a motorcycle accident, but not given the details of the accident.

15. T

16. F   A pseudonym is a name adopted by one who wishes to hide his or her identity. The lecturer does not indicate what pseudonym Lawrence adopted.

17. F   Lawrence *was* a living legend of *his* time.

LECTURE 10 MODEL AND EXERCISE

The Dust Bowl: Nature Against Mankind

One of the more tragic aspects of the *Depression years* of the 1930s in the United States was the weather. It seemed as though the weather was working directly against people. Floods and windstorms battered the northern and eastern sections of the country. At one time or another in the 1930s, most of the major rivers in the East rose over their banks and flooded the streets of eastern cities and towns. In fact, one flood, the Ohio River Flood of 1937, was one of the worst in the nation's history. It destroyed the homes of a half-million people. All in all, floods and windstorms in the 1930s took the lives of 3,678 people in the eastern part of the United States alone.

The weather was a major problem, not just in the North and in the East. During the '30s throughout the entire United States winters were unusually cold, and summers were unusually hot. In the summer of 1936, the farm state of Kansas had almost sixty days straight of 100° Fahrenheit heat. That's 37.7° Celsius. On July 24, 1936, the temperature reached 120° Fahrenheit. That's 49° on the Celsius scale. All throughout the western states, crops burned up, and people were miserable. One of the worst problems of the time for the western

United States was the combination of heat, *drought,* and the strong, hot, dusty winds which were known as black blizzards. People and animals suffered unbearably from the heat and the black blizzards. Farm crops were ruined by the drought.

Let's back up for a moment and take a look at what had been going on in the Great Plains area before the drought, heat, and blizzards hit. For years conservationists had warned that an *ecological catastrophe* was coming over the *Great Plains* of the United States. Nature had fooled us, they said, and we had overworked the land. They noted that, generally, the Great Plains area received about twenty inches or fifty-one centimeters of rain each year. This was the expected amount of annual rainfall. Because of this *meager*—this small—amount of yearly rainfall, 100 counties in the states of Colorado, Kansas, New Mexico, Texas, and Oklahoma had been called the "*Dust Bowl*" even in the 1920s. But, strangely, just before the Depression years of the 1930s, the Great Plains region had received extraordinarily heavy rains. This increase in the amount of precipitation increased farming in the Plains area. Many new small farms were established. Not only that, many of the new farmers allowed their cattle to *overgraze* the land, and they themselves *overplowed* the land. As a result, the cover vegetation of the land was severely damaged, and the topsoil was left exposed in many cases. In 1934 government conservationists estimated that 35 million acres of *arable land* had been completely destroyed because of overgrazing and overplowing; that's 14,164,000 hectares completely destroyed by poor farming practices. It was also estimated that another 100 million acres or 40,469,000 hectares of arable land were doomed by this misuse, this abuse of the land.

Then came a severe drought over the Plains area. The rains stopped coming. The amount of precipitation fell drastically. All of a sudden, in the early 1930s, the Dust Bowl grew from 100 counties in five states in the 1920s to 756 counties in 19 states in the '30s. Like Ireland in the 1800s, the Great Plains of the U.S. were threatened with famine, and its people with starvation.

Along with the drought and the heat came the dust storms or what were called black blizzards. The first of the blizzards struck in November, 1933 in the state of South Dakota. The farm soil began blowing away in the morning. It was reported that, by noon, the sky was blacker than night. When the sun finally reappeared, farm fields had been replaced by sand. Roads, trees, fences, and farm machinery had disappeared under great hills or dunes of sand. Winds blowing over the dry, bare fields piled sand as high as thirty feet—or nine meters. Some of the clouds of dust from the storms were five miles high. Imagine, a dust cloud eight kilometers high!

The second storm struck the state of Texas. Again, farms were changed into shifting Sahara Deserts. Farmers' wives packed every windowsill, door frame, and keyhole with oiled cloth to keep out the dust and the sand, but it still penetrated and lay in piles on the floors. During another of the black blizzards in the state of Oklahoma, street lights had to be kept on day and night for three weeks straight. Oklahomans had to wear dust masks when they went outside the house, and to add to their misery, the temperature stayed at 108° Fahrenheit, or if you prefer, 42.2° Celsius.

Because of this deadly combination of heat, drought, and black blizzards, many of the Great Plains farmers were ruined—especially the little farmers. The "For Sale" signs in front of their small farms marked the start of the Dust Bowl migrations. Counties in the Dust Bowl area lost 60 percent of their population because of migration. In one Texas county alone, the population dropped from 40,000 to 1,000 people. Among the most unfortunate of all the migrants who were forced to abandon their farms were the Oklahoma farmers. They were called "*Okies.*" Their misfortune and hardships were written about by the famous American novelist John Steinbeck in his book, *The Grapes of Wrath.* In 1940 an American movie of the same name portrayed the misery these poor Dust Bowl farmers suffered. You see, when their farms were ruined, many of the Okies moved to California, which they thought would be the "Promised Land." They hoped to find work and a better way of life in California. But what they actually found when they reached their "Promised Land" was just more *drudgery,* more hardship, and incredible poverty.

It's important to point out that not just the Okies suffered severe economic hardship during the years of the Depression. Many, many Americans from all areas of the country suffered. Yes, the years of the Depression were some of the most difficult the United States has ever experienced. They were years that saw both natural as well as economic disaster strike the country.

Key to Preview of Vocabulary (Lecture 10)

1. Depression years
2. Great Plains
3. drought
4. Dust Bowl
5. meager
6. ecological catastrophe
7. arable land
8. overplow
9. overgraze
10. drudgery
11. Okies

Key to Multiple-Choice Questions (Lecture 10)

1. How many people lost their lives because of floods and windstorms in the 1930s?　(a)
2. In Kansas in the summer of 1936, what was the temperature in degrees Celsius for sixty days straight?　(b)
3. When did the temperature reach 49 degrees on the Celsius scale in Kansas?　(d)
4. According to government estimates, how many acres of arable land had been completely destroyed by overplowing and overgrazing in the early 1930s?　(b)
5. How many hectares of arable land were doomed according to government estimates?　(d)
6. In terms of acres, what are 14,164,000 hectares equivalent to?　(b)
7. How many more Dust Bowl states were there in the 1930s than there were in the 1920s?　(c)
8. What was the percent increase in the number of counties included in the Dust Bowl area from the 1920s to the 1930s?　(d)
9. What was the height in metric measure of the giant dust cloud that was mentioned in the lecture?　(a)
10. What was the temperature in degrees Fahrenheit during the three-week Oklahoma black blizzard?　(d)
11. How much of a percentage drop in population did counties in the Dust Bowl region experience?　(c)
12. How many people emigrated from the Texas county mentioned in the lecture?　(c)
13. What is *The Grapes of Wrath*?　(c)
14. Why did the Okies migrate to California?　(d)

Key to True–False Statements (Lecture 10)

1. F　The weather seemed to be working *against,* not with, human beings.
2. ?　The lecturer indicated that the Ohio River Flood occurred in 1937 and that it was one of the worst floods in history, but he gave no indication of how long it lasted.
3. T
4. F　Winters were unusually cold, but summers were unusually *hot.*
5. T　(By inference.)
6. F　They were more than likely unhappy about the fact. They *warned* that an ecological *catastrophe* was coming over the Great Plains area.
7. ?　You have no way of determining that conservationists met with groups of small farmers from the information that was presented.
8. F　Just before the Depression years began, the expected amount of rainfall was much less than the amount of received rainfall in the Great Plains.
9. T
10. T
11. T
12. F　It was applied to *poor* people.
13. T

LECTURE 11 OVERVIEW

John F. Kennedy: Promise and Tragedy

SCRIPT

The lecturer starts off by pointing out that John Kennedy has been honored in death more than he ever was in life, and that his murder became a symbol of the tragedy and sometimes senselessness of life.

To begin with, she describes Kennedy as a surprising man. By this is meant that Kennedy did things earlier than other people do them. She gives you a few examples of the kinds of things he did earlier than others did.

Kennedy suffered some mishaps and tragedies in his life, and the lecturer is going to be talking about two of these mishaps and tragedies: his back injury and the death of his infant son.

The next topic that is discussed is Kennedy's decision making, and, I must say, it seems that he made most of his decisions alone, relying on his own judgment, after talking and conferring with his brother, Robert Kennedy, and his other advisers. We don't really know, for instance, why Kennedy made certain decisions about the Bay of Pigs; the Cuban missile crises; U.S. involvement in Vietnam; or the atomic test ban treaty.

Kennedy's idealism and perhaps his lack of realism is next touched upon in the lecture. Several examples of this are given. Let me here just mention (1) the condition of NATO—the North Atlantic Treaty Organization; (2) the Alliance for Progress; and (3) the creation of the Peace Corps, which, as you may know, was created to make American technical skills available to the developing countries of the world.

After that, the lecturer is going to talk about Kennedy's effectiveness in the world of international diplomacy as opposed to his apparent ineffectiveness in the world of American domestic politics. First, she lists his successes in Congress. They include: (1) the creation of the Peace Corps; (2) the raising of the minimum wage for workers; (3) the increase of social security benefits for America's senior citizens; and (4) financial support for space exploration. As for Kennedy's domestic failures: well, first Congress refused to pass bills on free medical care for people sixty-five years and older; second, it refused to create a department of urban affairs to help America's troubled cities; third, it also refused to pass Kennedy's proposal on federal aid to education; and last, it rejected his tax reform and reduction plan. When he was killed, Kennedy's whole domestic program was in trouble.

The next part of the lecture briefly discusses what Kennedy did to help Black people in the U.S. He was responsible for the bill that prohibits racial discrimination in the job market and in public facilities, and he is, perhaps most important of all, responsible for the bill that outlawed school segregation in the United States.

She finishes up the talk about John Kennedy's strengths and weaknesses, his successes and failures, his idealism and lack of realism, with a famous quotation from one of Kennedy's speeches, and I think this quote can apply to foreign students with regard to their countries as it applied to Americans and the U.S. Kennedy said, and I quote, "Ask not what your country can do for you; ask what you can do for your country." End quote. All right, now let's get down to the actual lecture. Are you ready to take notes?

LECTURE 11 NOTE-TAKING EXERCISE

John F. Kennedy: Promise and Tragedy

SCRIPT

It seems that John Fitzgerald Kennedy has been honored after his death as he never was during his life. Along with such men as George Washington, Abraham Lincoln, and Thomas Jefferson, he has been given a place in legend. Kennedy's murder in November of 1963—only two years and ten months after he became president—has become a symbol of the tragedy and the senselessness of life.

Kennedy was quite a surprising person. He never did things when others were doing them. Let me give you a few examples of what I mean. He went to Congress and to the White House earlier than most people. He was only twenty-nine years old when he won his first political election in 1947. He was elected president of the United States when he was only forty-three years old. At the age of forty-six, he was *assassinated.* Yes, Kennedy was the youngest man ever to be elected president of the United States, and, sadly, he was the youngest man ever to die in that office. He was also the first American president born in the 1900s.

Although Kennedy was young, well-educated, and rich, things did not always go smoothly for him. He suffered a series of *mishaps* and tragedies during his life. Let me cite just a few of these misfortunes. During World War II, he suffered a serious back injury. He had major surgery in 1954 and again in 1955 to correct the injury; however, his back bothered him for the rest of his life. While he was president, his son died soon after birth. His life was a mixture of political triumph and personal misfortune.

To judge Kennedy's 1,000 days in the White House is not easy. One of the reasons is that for a man who had such a keen sense of history, he was really quite disorderly about keeping records of what influenced and led up to his own political decisions. It is said that he often made these decisions alone after a series of private talks with his many advisers and with his younger brother Robert Kennedy (who was also assassinated—in 1968). From the numerous accounts of the Kennedy years, it seems that none of these advisers actually took part in the whole process of Kennedy's decision making. Apparently he spent very little time talking to even his closest associates about how he made final decisions. As a result, we don't have the full story on the two Cuban crises—the disastrous invasion of the Bay of Pigs in 1961, and the Russian attempt to install missiles in Cuba in 1962. We also don't know why, during his administration, the United States became more and more deeply involved in the civil war in Vietnam. We don't even have all the background on what led up to the atomic test ban treaty of 1963. You may remember that under this treaty, the United States, England, and the U.S.S.R. agreed not to test any more nuclear weapons in the earth's atmosphere, in outer space, or under water. I guess we could say that Kennedy relied heavily on his own judgment in making policy decisions. Many of these decisions reflect Kennedy's idealism—and, sometimes, his lack of realism.

In his handling of American foreign policy, for instance, Kennedy *envisioned* a strong, interdependent Atlantic world—that was his ideal—but the reality was something else. For example, the North Atlantic Treaty Organization (or NATO) was in rather poor shape during most of his administration. Only three years after Kennedy's death, France withdrew from the military affairs of NATO. In Latin America, he won admiration with his plans for the Alliance for Progress, but again, as any Latin American will tell you, the Alliance was much more a dream than a reality. One of his more successful idealistic plans was the creation of the Peace Corps which was supposed to make American technical skills available to some of the developing countries.

But because of this idealism, his youth, and his personal charm, I think most people would agree on one thing. President Kennedy was a lot more effective in the world of international diplomacy than he ever was in the world of American domestic politics. He enjoyed meeting with the heads of foreign countries and with foreign students at the White House, and he had a rare combination of informality and dignity that made him very effective in this role. But to make small-talk—to *chit-chat*—with self-important American Congressmen really bored him, and he simply would not take the time to do it, as his successor, President Lyndon Johnson, did with such political success. Kennedy and the American Congress did not get along well. As a result, Kennedy had a great deal of difficulty getting his domestic programs approved by Congress. The "New Frontier," as his administration was called, had some successes in its first year. For example, Congress established the Peace Corps; it raised the *minimum wage* from $1.00 to $1.25 per hour. (The minimum wage is the least amount of money per hour that a worker can be paid.) Today, by the way, the minimum wage is $3.50 per hour. Congress also increased *social security benefits*—which is money that is paid to people sixty-five years and older. Kennedy also succeeded in getting more money for space exploration programs. During his administration, American astronauts made their first space flights and began their preparation to send men to the moon. Just six years after Kennedy's death the first man actually landed on the moon.

However, the Congress refused to pass many proposals that Kennedy suggested. Let me list just a few of these proposals: (1) free medical care for people over sixty-five; (2) the creation of a department of urban affairs—American cities were in a state of decay; (3) federal aid to education; and (4) tax reform and tax reduction. It's quite possible that, because the country was experiencing general prosperity, it was difficult to convince the Congress or the American people of the need for serious social and political change in the U.S. When Kennedy was assassinated in 1963, his entire domestic program was in big trouble.

And yet, part of the Kennedy legend is connected with his introduction of the most radical legislation affecting the Black Americans in the United States in this century. He was responsible for the bill that prohibited *discrimination,* in this case racial discrimination, in employment, and in public facilities such as public transportation, in restaurants, and restrooms, and so on. He was also responsible for the bill that outlawed school *segregation.* This bill, however, was passed by Congress, but not until after Kennedy's death.

Although the promise and tragedy of John Kennedy was, in many ways, a lot greater than any of his actual accomplishments, the tragedy of his death resulted in definite social reform in the United States, and it left the hope that a youthful, idealistic person like John Kennedy will appear on the American political scene, another president who will remind the American people to "ask not what your country can do for you; ask what you can do for your country."

Key to Preview of Vocabulary (Lecture 11)

1. mishap
2. minimum wage
3. assassinated
4. discrimination
5. segregation
6. chit-chat
7. envision
8. social security benefits

Key to Multiple-Choice Questions (Lecture 11)

1. How many months did John Kennedy serve as President of the United States?   (d)
2. How many years passed between the time Kennedy won his first Congressional election and the presidential election?   (b)
3. How old was Kennedy when he was assassinated?   (d)
4. In what years did Kennedy undergo major back operations?   (d)
5. How many years after Kennedy was killed was his brother assassinated? (b)
6. Which of the following countries did not sign the atomic test ban treaty of 1963?   (b)
7. In his handling of American foreign policy, which of the following was not a major concern of John Kennedy?   (c)
8. In what year did France withdraw from the military affairs of NATO?   (d)

9. When did the first man land on the moon?   (d)
10. Which of the following Kennedy proposals was not passed by Congress when he was alive?   (b)
11. For whose benefit did John Kennedy introduce the most radical legislation in the United States in the twentieth century?   (a)

Key to True–False Statements (Lecture 11)

1. T
2. F   Kennedy's murder took place in the *fall* of 1963.
3. ?   The lecturer did not touch upon this point.
4. F   The lecturer stated that "although Kennedy was young, well-educated, and rich, things did *not* always go smoothly for him."
5. ?   It was mentioned that his newborn son died, but no date for the death was given.
6. F   Kennedy apparently spent very *little* time talking to even his closest advisers about how he made final decisions.
7. F   Kennedy had such a keen (acute) sense of history, *but* he was really quite disorderly about keeping records of what influenced and led up to his political decisions.
8. T
9. T
10. T
11. F   The "New Frontier" refers to Kennedy's administration, his term in office.
12. T   "Senior citizens" are people over sixty-five years of age.
13. T
14. T
15. F   Kennedy is famous for the remark that Americans should not ask what *their country can do for them,* but *what they can do for their country.* This is just the opposite of the remark in the true–false statement.

LECTURE 12 OVERVIEW

The End of an Empire: Montezuma and Cortes

The first part of the lecture is organized chronologically. Quite a few dates are given, and you should note down all these dates and the events that took place at these times. The lecturer will begin the talk by describing when and where the Aztec Empire existed. He will also describe how large it was and tell you something about its military power and its leader, Montezuma. He will then touch upon the coming of the Spaniards into the empire with the arrival of two Spanish ships and the strange-looking soldiers that came out of these ships. As the Spaniards advanced toward the capital city, they met no military resistance from Montezuma because he thought that Cortes was a returning Aztec god.

SCRIPT

The lecturer then will spend some time telling about how the Spaniards entered the capital city and took the king prisoner. It was about seven months later that the Aztecs rebelled against the Spaniards. At this time many Spanish soldiers and many Indians were killed. Montezuma also died in the fight. The capital city finally fell to the Spaniards and was completely destroyed.

At this point in the lecture, the speaker will shift from giving a chronological listing of events to showing a reason-result—a cause-and-effect—relationship between these events. He will bring to light some of the more obvious reasons why such a small band of Spanish adventurers could bring about the fall of the mighty, militaristic Aztec Empire. He will allude to Montezuma's fear of the supernatural, in other words, his fear that Cortes was a god. Second, it will be mentioned that the Spaniards had superior weapons to fight against the Indians with—the Spaniards had guns. The Indians did not. They had only clubs and spears. The lecturer will also be describing how the Spaniards used Indians to fight Indians, and made good use of the old idea of "divide and conquer" in war. Lastly, it will be noted that at the very heart of the conquest and fall of the empire was the human desire for riches—for gold and silver—and for conquest. He will end up the lecture by noting that although the Aztec Empire was destroyed, another nation and culture did develop out of the union of Indian and European cultures. I'm referring, of course, to the Republic of Mexico.

LECTURE 12 NOTE-TAKING EXERCISE

The End of an Empire: Montezuma and Cortes

SCRIPT

During the fifteenth century—to be more specific, between the years 1423 and 1440—the Aztec Indians built the most powerful empire ever known in Mexico. The Aztecs had *subjugated* and dominated the entire area that is today Mexico City. At one time the Aztec Empire extended from Mexico City as far south as Guatemala. The capital city of the empire, Tenochtitlan, contained beautiful buildings, well-stocked marketplaces, and the remarkable pyramid-temples. On the *altars* of these temples, thousands of human sacrifices to the Aztec gods were made. Some of these human sacrifices, usually Indian prisoners of war, had their hearts literally ripped out of their bodies.

Some 300,000 people lived in the Aztec capital. It was, in fact, one of the largest cities in the sixteenth-century world. It was five times larger than sixteenth-century London. The Aztecs were fierce fighters and the capital city of their empire was indeed a *military fortress* filled with soldiers. You know, the military intelligence system of the empire was so amazingly effective that their leader Montezuma knew that strange men—the Spaniards—were approaching his capital city long before they were anywhere near it. He also knew exactly how the Spanish soldiers rode horses and how they fired guns. Montezuma, by the way, ruled between the years 1480 and 1520.

And yet, in spite of this early warning system, an army of only 553 Spanish soldiers managed to conquer the most powerful, advanced militaristic empire of the New World. How, indeed, was this possible? Why did it happen? Let's go back a bit . . .

In the spring of the year 1519, an Indian runner from the Gulf Coast area of the Aztec Empire gave a strange report to Montezuma. He said that he had seen two floating mountains—they were, of course, the Spanish ships—and that out of these floating mountains, strangely-dressed men had come—these men were the Spanish soldiers. The Indian said that the men had beards and that their skin was very white. When the emperor heard this report, he nervously remembered the Aztec legend of the bearded, light-skinned god, Quetzalcoatl. According to the legend this god was supposed to return to earth one day to claim his kingdom which was, at that time, the Aztec Empire. So, Montezuma mistakenly, but perhaps understandably, *assumed* that Hernan Cortes, the leader of the soldiers of Spain, was the expected god, Quetzalcoatl. So he offered no resistance whatsoever to the approaching Spaniard and his small army. Instead, he sent presents of gold and silver to the approaching conquistadores. He asked them politely to leave his empire, but when the Spaniards saw the presents of gold and silver, they were even more excited and determined to conquer this empire for Spain and, of course, to steal its gold and silver.

In November of 1519, the Spaniards entered the capital city and took the emperor Montezuma prisoner. It was not until June of 1520 that the Aztecs rebelled against the small army of Spaniards. Montezuma was killed during this rebellion. He was, so the story goes, stoned to death by his own people, but no one really knows whether it was the Spaniards or the Aztecs who caused Montezuma's death. Many Spanish soldiers were killed on what has been named *la noche triste*—"the sorrowful night"—which occurred on June 30 in 1520.

Cortes, who had been away from the capital at the start of the uprising, returned and attacked the city. According to Cortes's own figures, on one day of fighting for the capture of the Aztec capital, 40,000 Aztecs died; on another 12,000 were killed; and on another day of the battle 6,000 were killed by Spanish guns. The Indians, you see, were fighting with clubs and spears; the Spaniards with guns. The battle went on for seventy-five days, and finally on August 31, 1520 the greatest city of the Aztec Empire fell and was completely destroyed. Cortes founded Mexico City on its *ruins*.

Again, the question arises: how could an expedition of only 553 Spaniards manage to conquer the most powerful, war-like empire of the New World? Well, as I already mentioned, the *prophecy* of a returning god completely *immobilized* the leader of the empire. Montezuma didn't know exactly what to do as he awaited the arrival of what he thought was a god. Furthermore, this god was accompanied by an army of gods who could fire flashes of lightning. (Remember, the Aztecs had never seen guns.) To make matters worse, the gods seemed to be half man and half animal. (The Spaniards rode on horses—the Aztecs had also never seen horses before.) To the Indians, the Spaniards must have looked like what men from Mars would look like to us today!

Another important factor in the Aztecs' conquest was Cortes's use of Indian allies. He used Indian against Indian, so to speak. Cortes convinced the various Indian tribes to ally themselves with him against their hated enemies, the Aztecs. So, all along his march from the sea, Cortes gathered Indian allies until his small expedition of 553 Spanish adventurers increased to an army of over 75,000 fighting men. His success in gathering Indian allies was largely due to an Indian woman known as La Malinche. That's spelled L–a M–a–l–i–n–c–h–e. La Malinche, who was also called Doña Marina, spoke the languages of both the Aztec and Mayan Indians. As a result, Cortes, through her, could communicate in the two major Indian languages. So, she was a great help to Cortes in his *negotiations* with the Indians and even with the emperor Montezuma himself. In effect, she helped bring about the fall of the Aztec Empire.

And so we can perhaps sum up some of the major factors involved in the conquest of one of the greatest empires ever known: well, to begin with, I'll cite man's fear of the supernatural—the fear of the appearance of a legendary god; second, let me cite the Spaniards' military superiority in the area of weapons—Spanish guns as opposed to Indian clubs; third, the tool of political *intrigue*—the turning of Indian against Indian; and last, but certainly not of least importance, the human thirst for adventure and the factor of human greed—the conquistadores were seeking gold and silver, and they did not care in the least if an empire and a culture were completely destroyed to satisfy their greed. All these factors and some others not even touched upon here led to the downfall of the mighty Aztec Empire. And yet, after its fall, another nation emerged, one which turned out to be a *fusion* of Indian and European culture. This cultural fusion eventually led to the overthrow of colonial rule and to the establishment of the Republic of Mexico.

Key to Preview of Vocabulary (Lecture 12)

1. altar
2. assumes
3. subjugate
4. ruins
5. immobilized

6. negotiations
7. military fortress
8. prophecy
9. intrigue
10. fusion

Key to Multiple-Choice Questions (Lecture 12)

1. Between what years did the Aztecs build the most powerful empire ever known in the Americas?   (b)
2. What was the population of Tenochtitlan during the sixteenth century?   (d)
3. From the information given, what was the population of London, England in the sixteenth century?   (b)
4. For how long did Montezuma rule the Aztec Empire?   (c)
5. How did Montezuma react when he first learned that Spanish soldiers were approaching his capital?   (d)
6. When did the Spaniards take Montezuma prisoner?   (b)
7. When did the Aztec rebellion against the Spanish occupation occur?   (a)
8. According to Cortes, how many Indians were killed in the battle for the Aztec capital?   (d)
9. How long did the battle for the capital last?   (b)
10. How many Spanish conquistadores were there in Cortes's expedition when it first started out in the New World?   (b)
11. Why was Cortes, in all probability, successful in gathering Indian allies to fight against the Aztecs?   (c)
12. How large an army finally attacked the Aztec capital?   (d)
13. What factors led to the downfall of the Aztec Empire?   (d)

Key to True–False Statements (Lecture 12)

1. F   They built the most powerful empire in what is today Mexico.
2. T
3. F   They believed in offering human sacrifices to their gods.
4. ?   Nowhere in the lecture is it mentioned where the prisoners were housed.
5. T
6. T
7. F   If the Spaniards had killed most of the Indians they met, they would have had no allies.
8. T   One can assume this because they were so surprised to see white, bearded men.
9. T   Erroneously = mistakenly. Cortes was no god.
10. F   Montezuma sent gold and silver to the Spaniards.
11. F   They rebelled *seven* months later.
12. T
13. ?   One might imagine that he did, but there is no way of knowing whether he did or did not receive good treatment from the Spaniards.
14. F   Military superiority benefited the cause of the *Spaniards.*
15. F   He was immobilized with fear that Cortes was a god, so he did nothing at first.

16. F   They had never seen guns *or* horses before.

17. T   One can assume so since the Aztecs captured area Indians and used them for sacrifices.

18. T   This is no doubt why she could negotiate between the Spaniards, the area Indians, and the Aztecs.

19. F   The small band of 553 Europeans had grown to a fighting force of more than 75,000 fighting men. Many area Indians fought against the Aztecs.

20. ?   This is nowhere stated or implied in the lecture information.

LECTURE 13 OVERVIEW

Language: Origin and Diversity

In this lecture about the origin and diversity of our system of communication—language—one of the speakers will begin by remarking that communication is common to both animals and humans. He will give several examples of animals communicating messages through actions or gestures, sounds, and smells; however, he will emphasize that human beings, unlike the animals, can carry a message or a communication far beyond the immediate situation or time that the message is given in. Further detail about this point will be given during the presentation. After this he will define just exactly what language is and he'll say something about the different forms our system of communication takes, but he will state that he's going to be dealing with a discussion of our spoken language in this lecture—not with our written or sign language. Anyway, he will talk briefly about the mystery that surrounds the origin of language. You see, it's not really known for sure whether at one time all our different modern languages had one common source or whether they developed from different sources in different places during our prehistory—that's, of course, the time before written records of language were kept. He will point out that attempts have been made to trace the history of our languages with a system known as comparative linguistics. He will cite the tracing of most of the languages used in the Western world today to the unrecorded source or parent language called Proto-Indo-European. At this point in the talk, I'll begin to list some of the modern languages spoken today and indicate the approximate number of speakers who use the language as a first language, according to some recent language statistics. You should note down all of these statistics on the number of speakers of each language. This will test your ability to get down numbers that are given in fairly rapid succession. Most of these numbers will fall, understandably, into the millions category; but let me also point out here that in the entire world today there are really only thirteen languages that are spoken by groups of people numbering more than fifty million. Some languages are spoken by small groups of people numbering only a few hundred or a few thousand. Can you guess where people who speak such languages live? Well, I'll let you know. O.K. The first speaker will end up with a brief discussion of the attempt to develop an artificial "universal" language. You may have heard of Esperanto, the synthetic language developed for international communication purposes. Well, it really hasn't solved the problem of our many and varied languages. This is partly because Esperanto is mostly based on Western European language structure and vocabulary. The only solution, for the present, it seems, is to do just what you are doing right now—learning a second language in order to communicate with people who do not speak your native language. How are you doing with your endeavor?

Let's move on now.

LECTURE 13 NOTE-TAKING EXERCISE

Language: Origin and Diversity

As we all know, both humans and animals communicate with their own *species,* but, unlike us, animals do not communicate with words and sentences; they use signals, such as gestures, sounds, and smells. For instance, a dog barks to show excitement, but it snarls to show annoyance or anger. A cat purrs to indicate contentment. Gorillas will shake their heads from side to side to show that they mean no harm, but their steady stare is a definite threat or warning. To be sure, an animal can show joy, anger, dislike, or even fear through its voice and actions, but it seems that the animal cannot carry its message of anger, fear, and so forth beyond the immediate situation. Human beings, on the other hand, can. We mean by this that we can refer to the present, the past, or to the future. We can deal with what is out of sight and with what is millions of miles away. We can even communicate through writing or a tape recording with grandchildren who are born only after we are dead. To do all this, we use language.

Now, in a general sense, language is any form of expression used for communication. This would include writing, sign language, music, dance, and painting; however, we are going to focus our discussion on the basic form of language, which is, of course, speech. It is a fact that no human group is without speech, even though some groups do lack a writing system to record their speech. So it is safe to say that all humans combine sound and meaning into a complex *code* of communication. This code is their language.

`SCRIPT`

When, where, and how language began is still a deep mystery, although there are many theories on the subject—some of them quite funny. The problem is that there are no written records of any language that are more than several thousand years old. To the best of our knowledge, the oldest writing was done approximately 5,000 years ago in *Sumerian,* the language of ancient *Mesopotamia*—a region that has become part of modern Iraq. And so, we cannot really know for sure whether at one time all our different modern languages—which number about three thousand—did have one common source or whether they developed from different sources in different places during our *prehistory.* Yet, it has been possible to trace the history of our languages down through the centuries by examining the similarities and differences that exist among today's various languages. This examination is called *comparative linguistics.*

Most of the languages used in the Western world today have been traced to the common, yet unrecorded, source which linguists call *Proto-Indo-European.* The languages descended from this parent language, which was spoken as far back as 4000 B.C., include nearly all those major languages spoken in Europe and in both North and South America. Certain Persian languages as well as several of India's chief languages have also been traced to Proto-Indo-European.

As for the major languages of the Far East—Chinese and *Polynesian*—there are more speakers of the languages of this region than there are speakers of Russian, Arabic, and the various Western languages put together. While Russian is spoken by about 140 million people, Chinese is spoken by approximately 800 million people. The latest statistics show that the world's population is over 3.5 billion and growing, and it has been estimated that the Chinese languages are gaining approximately 14 million speakers each year. Arabic, which belongs to another historically important family—the *Afro-Asiatic family*—is spoken by 115 million people, mainly in the Middle East and North Africa.

Let's put aside language families for awhile and talk about some of the various languages that are spoken by large groups of people today. There's Japanese, spoken by 105 million people; French, spoken by 55 million people; German—120 million; and Italian, with 60 million speakers. The Persian language is spoken by 25 million people while Vietnamese and Thai are spoken by 35 million and 29 million people, respectively. Finally, 184 million people speak the major language of India, Hindi. Let me emphasize, however, that it is always difficult to get accurate language statistics of any kind.

As for English, well, today it seems to have replaced French as the world's *lingua franca.* It is spoken and understood by nearly 317 million people as a first language. It has become the most common second language for many millions of people all over the world. The next most popular second language for millions of people is Spanish. It is spoken by at least 180 million people as a first language.

As I previously pointed out, the peoples of the world speak about 3,000 different languages. One linguist has put the number at 2,796 languages. It is true, however, that many of these languages are spoken by small groups of people numbering only a few hundred or a few thousand. For example, Spanish almost completely replaced the languages of the small groups of South American natives, while English has replaced many of the languages of North America. And yet, more than 1,000 languages are still spoken by different tribes of North American Indians. Approximately another 1,000 languages are spoken by small African and Asian groups. Actually, there are really only thirteen languages in the world today that are spoken by groups numbering more than fifty million people.

Because of all this linguistic diversity in the world, it is no wonder that people have been so *intrigued* by the idea of developing an artificial "universal" language. At various times in the history of the Western world, there have been several attempts to develop just such a language. The most well-known attempt was the development of *Esperanto*. This *synthetic* language was devised in the late nineteenth century by a Polish scientist, Dr. L. Zamenhof; however, for the most part, Esperanto has not really been very widely used, probably because it is based mostly on Western European language structure and vocabulary, and so it is certainly as difficult for speakers of Arabic, Russian, Chinese, and Japanese to learn as it is for them to learn French, German, or English. And so, until a workable artificial universal language is developed and perfected, we will be forced to learn a foreign, or shall we say, a second language, in order to communicate with people who do not speak our native language.

Key to Preview of Vocabulary (Lecture 13)

1. Mesopotamia
2. species
3. code
4. Sumerian
5. Proto-Indo-European
6. comparative linguistics
7. prehistory
8. Afro-Asiatic family
9. Polynesian
10. *lingua franca*
11. intrigued
12. Esperanto; synthetic

Key to Multiple-Choice Questions (Lecture 13)

1. What is the basic form of human language?   (b)
2. To the best of our knowledge, when was the oldest writing done?   (d)

3. How has man been able to trace the history of language down through the centuries?   (c)
4. Which of the following languages is descended from Proto-Indo-European?   (d)
5. Approximately how many people speak Russian?   (c)
6. How many fewer speakers of Russian than Chinese are there?   (c)
7. Which of the languages mentioned in the lecture is spoken by 115 million people?   (a)
8. What is the estimated total number of speakers of Japanese?   (d)
9. Which language mentioned is spoken by 25 million people?   (b)
10. In total, how many people speak Thai and Vietnamese?   (c)
11. The major language of India, Hindi, is spoken by how many speakers? (c)
12. Which of the world's languages is spoken by more than 317 million speakers as a first language?   (a)
13. According to this lecture, what is the second most popular second language?   (d)
14. What has one linguist estimated to be the exact number of languages spoken by various groups of people all over the world? . (a)
15. How many first languages are actually spoken by more than 50 million people?   (a)

Key to True–False Statements (Lecture 13)

1. F   Communication is common to both humans and animals.
2. F   A gorilla will shake its head to show that it means no harm.
3. F   Animals can express joy, anger, dislike, and fear.
4. ?   Nowhere in the lecture is this information indicated.
5. T
6. F   *Speech* is the basic form of all language.
7. T
8. T
9. T
10. T
11. F   Proto-Indo-European has been designated as the parent language of the modern languages of Europe, North and South America, Iran, and India only.
12. T
13. F   More people speak the languages of the Far East—Chinese and Polynesian—than any other.
14. F   They certainly are *not* accurate and reliable. They are just estimates.
15. ?   This cannot be deduced from the information given.
16. F   At various times in the history of the *Western* world, there have been attempts made to create an artificial "universal" language.
17. F   It is quite difficult for a speaker of Arabic or Russian to learn Esperanto because it is based on the Western European language structure.

LECTURE 14 NOTE-TAKING EXERCISE

The World's Changing Climate: Fire or Ice?

Let me begin this commentary on the world's changing climate by saying that climatology, the study of long-range trends in weather, is at best an inexact science. It is based on hypotheses. Currently, a major argument among climatologists concerns the long-range weather outlook for the earth. The question that occupies them so much is this: Is the earth cooling off, or is it in fact heating up? Is the earth going through a cooling trend or a warming trend? A cooling trend could bring mass starvation and fuel shortages. But on the other hand, a warming trend could melt the polar ice caps and cause flooding of the coastal cities of the world. In either case, the consequences for man might be alarming, and possibly disastrous. Let me just point out that rains and floods of record proportions have recently struck some geographic areas around the world while droughts have devastated other areas. So let's take a look at the various parts of the world to see exactly what has been happening lately in terms of the earth's weather conditions.

The continent of Africa, up until 1974, had six consecutive years of drought. In the great drought of 1972–74, as many as 500,000 people died. Since 1974, there has, indeed, been rain, but it has proved to be both a blessing and a problem for the Africans. This is because along with the rainfall has come a plague of rats, locusts, and caterpillars which, in some parts of the continent, have eaten everything in sight.

Now let's take a look at the continent of Asia. Although Asia has recently seen the strengthening of the monsoons in most parts of India and Pakistan, the present climatological trend seems to indicate that the monsoon pattern, which is quite complex, is being disrupted in Asia. Monsoon, by the way, comes from an Arabic word. Now, the monsoon lands of the world are regions that are exposed to seasonally alternating winds. These winds are powered by the annual variations in the temperature differences between the continents and the oceans. In summer, the winds blow from the ocean toward the continent. These summer winds bring the moist air from the ocean and cause the heavy rainfall. In winter, the opposite happens; the winds blow from the continent toward the ocean. This causes the dry season for the continent. So, as I said before, the monsoon lands of the world are those regions that are dry half of the year and that are wet the other half of the year. Now north of the monsoon regions, subtropical high pressure wind systems have produced the deserts of Asia and of North Africa, too. If these deserts should contract in the north and expand southward because of the earth's cooling—again, if the deserts of Asia and North Africa expand and move southward—the monsoons of Asia will be

SCRIPT

suppressed, and the entire Asian monsoon pattern will be disrupted and upset. If this happens, there are certain to be more droughts in Asia. The fact is that in the early 1900s there was a drought in Asia about every three or four years, but this was because the earth was warming up through the latter half of the nineteenth century and the first half of the twentieth century, so the monsoons were penetrating farther north on the Asian continent. As a result, drought frequency was declining to about one drought every eighteen years. In the past few decades, however, it appears that the deserts are pushing southward; so the present weather trend seems to be a return to a higher-frequency drought pattern for the Asian continent. In other words, Asia appears due for more droughts in the future.

The continent of Australia has also been hit by severe drought. In parts of its southern region, there has been no more than 10 percent of the normal yearly rainfall. In 1976, fodder for cattle was so scarce that Australian farmers killed the livestock they were unable to feed. In South Australia, farmers had to slaughter an estimated 10,000 head of cattle and 2,000,000 sheep to prevent overgrazing of the drought-stricken land.

Europe's climate has been undergoing abnormal conditions, too. The summer of 1976 was one of Western Europe's hottest and driest. England and parts of France, Belgium, Italy, and West Germany went months without rain. Fields dried up, and crops shriveled. Water transportation in Europe was also seriously affected. The levels of some German, English, and French rivers and canals dropped so low that ships and barges had to carry smaller cargo loads in order to be able to ride higher in the water. In France, with many rivers flowing at only one-third their normal level, hydroelectric power was greatly reduced, and because of this, French utilities had to burn 2,000,000 extra tons of oil in order to meet the country's electric power needs.

At the same time, the United States has also been undergoing some major climatic changes that could possibly result in another Dust Bowl for the country. In the past few years, the Midwest of the United States has been hit by severe drought. In the summer of 1976 in Wisconsin, crop losses due to drought were estimated at 400 million dollars. So we can see that food production certainly does depend on the variability of the weather.

Well, do all these climatic abnormalities mean that something drastic is happening to the global weather systems? Climatologists admit that they do not know for sure. A mere change of 2 degrees Centigrade (3.6 degrees Fahrenheit) in the annual average air temperature would indeed have profound effects for the earth. Higher temperatures might expand the deserts of the world and shorten crop-growing seasons. Lower temperatures would also affect crop growing. Between the years 1950 and 1977, for example, England's annual growing season shrank by nine or ten days because of lower temperatures. In the late spring of

1981 Britain was hit by the worst blizzards of the century, and temperatures were 10 degrees below normal for the springtime of the year.

Climatologists, in general, are truly puzzled by the changes taking place today. As I already said, some parts of the world are cooling off while others are growing warmer. Climatologists hope to discover why this is so and perhaps to predict what may come next. A number of climatologists believe the earth is, in fact, undergoing a cooling trend and is returning to the conditions of the "Little Ice Age." This "Little Ice Age" could best be described as the cold, damp weather that was characteristic of the period from approximately the fourteenth century to the mid-nineteenth century. Weather satellites indicate that the permanent snow and ice caps of both north and south poles have increased sharply; this would definitely signify a cooling trend for the earth. Reporting on the year 1972, one climatologist noted that the atmosphere in the Northern Hemisphere averaged 1 degree Centigrade or 1.80 degrees Fahrenheit colder than it did in 1949. On the other hand, other climatologists believe that the cooling trend is being offset by a warming trend. They believe that this warming trend is being caused by the increase of carbon dioxide in the atmosphere due to pollution from factories, cars, and so forth. The carbon dioxide level is already up more than 10 percent since 1850, and it is estimated that by the year 2000 it may have risen another 20 percent—enough to cause a 1-degree Fahrenheit (0.56 degree Centigrade) rise in average world temperatures. This large amount of carbon dioxide in the earth's atmosphere prevents some of the heat radiated by the surface of the earth from escaping out into space. This heat that is thus locked in, so to speak, is causing the heating up of the entire planet's atmosphere and is, inadvertently, changing the world's weather dynamics. And so, people are indeed a factor in today's weather equation—a crucial factor with our smog, our smoke, and our car exhausts.

No matter what else, both groups of climatologists do agree that, whatever the long-term trend in the earth's climate is, we are witnessing a period of increasing climatological change, a period that is making seasonal weather predictions and agricultural planning more and more difficult, if not altogether impossible.

Key to Multiple-Choice Questions (Lecture 14)

1. What happened to the continent of Africa in the great drought of 1972–1974?   (c)
2. What season in Asia is the rainy season?   (a)
3. What are the monsoon lands of the world?   (c)
4. What was the drought frequency pattern for Asia in the early 1900s?   (a)

5. How many cattle and sheep had to be put to death because of south Australia's severe drought?   (c)
6. French rivers were flowing at what percentage of their normal level during the summer of 1976?   (d)
7. How much extra oil had to be burned in France in order to meet the country's electric power needs in 1976?   (c)
8. In Wisconsin during the summer drought of 1976, how much did crop losses cost the people?   (c)
9. What could be said of Britain's spring weather of 1981?   (c)
10. When did the "Little Ice Age" occur?   (b)
11. How much colder in degrees Centigrade was the atmosphere of the Northern Hemisphere in 1972 than it was in 1949?   (b)
12. From 1850 to 2000 how much of a percentage increase in the carbon dioxide level has been predicted?   (c)

Key to True–False Statements (Lecture 14)

1. F   Climatology is an inexact science because it is based on hypotheses.
2. T
3. F   The rain was a problem because it brought a plague of rats and insects with it.
4. T
5. T
6. F   The winter monsoon winds bring the *dry* season to the Asian continent.
7. T
8. T
9. F   The continent of Asia has been hit by drought, and the continent of Australia has also been hit by drought.
10. T
11. T
12. T
13. F   They are not convinced that something drastic is happening.
14. F   Higher temperatures would cause the deserts of the world to *expand.*
15. F   Men and women are affecting the earth's weather dynamics because we are polluting the atmosphere.
16. T
17. F   They slaughtered the cattle to prevent overgrazing of the parched land.
18. ?   The fate of the rats and insects was not discussed.
19. ?   This is not mentioned by the lecturer.
20. ?   It is mentioned that weather satellites photograph the north and south poles, but the lecturer says nothing about the photography process.

LECTURE 15 NOTE-TAKING EXERCISE

The Egyptian Pyramids: Houses of Eternity

To many people throughout the world, some of the most remarkable and puzzling monuments of ancient times are the pyramids of ancient Egypt. You know, almost nothing at all remains of the once-great cities of the kings of Egypt, the pharoahs. Time and weather have been really hard on ancient Egypt's cities and towns, but several of the temples, statues, and, most important of all, the pyramids have survived. Even though many of the pyramids are in ruins, they still give us some idea of the magnificence of ancient Egypt's civilization—a civilization that, after all, lasted for more than 3,000 years. Remember, when we're talking about ancient Egypt, we're talking about at least thirty consecutive dynasties. A dynasty is a series of kings or queens of the same royal family—something like the Romanovs of Europe, the Ming Dynasty of China, or the Al-Sauds of Saudi Arabia.

As many of you probably already know, the pyramids were constructed as tombs or burial places for the Egyptian kings and their family members. You see, the ancient Egyptians passionately believed in life after death. In fact, their entire culture revolved around that belief. The kings, queens, and state officials often spent an entire lifetime preparing for their life after death. They did this by collecting possessions or "grave goods," by building tombs, and so forth. The Egyptians believed that they could be assured of an afterlife only if their bodies could be preserved from decay or destruction. So when a person died, and especially when a pharaoh died, in order to ensure his eternal life, he had his body embalmed or mummified. In other words, he had his corpse dried out and wrapped in linen to preserve it from decay. Then he had his mummy hidden. This whole idea may seem quite strange today, but the ancient Egyptians really believed that if one's mummy was destroyed, then his or her soul would be destroyed, and if, on the other hand, the mummy—the dead body—was preserved, the soul would be immortal. Let me repeat that. If one's mummy was destroyed, the soul would die. If the mummy was preserved, the soul would go on living.

For another thing, the ancient Egyptians believed that the dead person could take his or her earthly possessions along to the next world—this is just the opposite of the Western idea that "you can't take it with you when you go." Anyway, the dead person was provided with food, clothing, furniture, weapons, and even servants. It was not at all unusual for the pharaoh's slaves to be put to death so that they could serve him in his afterlife.

And so you can see why the pharaohs wanted to have their bodies and their possessions hidden to protect them from grave robbers. Before they died, they had special tombs built for this purpose—to hide their bodies and treasures. In the early years of ancient Egypt, these tombs were the pyramids—the vast burial chambers that were built to fool the grave robbers. Unfortunately, the grave robbers almost always outsmarted even the most powerful and the most careful of pharaohs. They broke into most of the pyramids or tombs and stole the gold and other treasures that they found. They even desecrated and destroyed the mummies of the dead. Needless to say, they would not bother a poor person's grave. These grave robbers even banded together into organizations or brotherhoods. Just imagine, a grave robbers' union!

Now, as for the actual construction of the mighty pyramids, it was during the First and Second Dynasties that the kings and nobles of Egypt began to construct the type of tomb called "the mastaba." The First and Second Dynasties lasted from about 3100 until 2665 B.C. Mastaba, by the way, comes from an Arabic word meaning "bench" or "long seat." A mastaba looked like a low, flat-topped rectangle—something like a low bench or a shoebox. Essentially, the pointed pyramid was no more than the extension upwards of the flat-topped mastaba.

The first "typical" pyramid (or, at least what most people generally think a pyramid looks like) was built during the Third Dynasty (which lasted roughly from about 2664 until 2615 B.C.). This pyramid was built for King Zoser (that's spelled Z–o–s–e–r) in about 2650 B.C. It was built by an architect named Imhotep (I–m–h–o–t–e–p). This pyramid was constructed as a series of giant steps or stairs. It, along with the others of its type, is called the Step Pyramid. It was really simply a pile of mastabas, each higher step smaller than the one before. The Step Pyramid of King Zoser was different from the later pyramids because it was never covered with stone to give it a smooth surface.

Actually, it was not until the Fourth Dynasty that the most famous pyramids were built. The three great pyramids of Giza belong to the Fourth Dynasty pyramids. (The Fourth Dynasty covered the period from 2614 to 2502 B.C.) They are located near the town of Giza, on the west bank of the Nile River, just outside the capital city of Egypt, Cairo. The Great Pyramids are really the very best preserved of all the Egyptian pyramids. The largest of these pyramids is known as the Great Pyramid. And great it is! It was built for King Khufu (that's K–h–u–f–u). (Khufu was called Cheops [C–h–e–o–p–s] by the Greeks, and so the pyramid is sometimes called the Pyramid of Cheops.) It has been estimated that 2,300,000 blocks of limestone were used to build the Great Pyramid. The blocks averaged 2,500 kilos each. The largest stone block weighs about 15,000 kilos. The base of the pyramid covers 5.3 hectares—an area large enough to hold ten football fields. There's a story that the conqueror Napoleon once sat in the shadow of the Great Pyramid and calculated that the mass of stone contained in the pyramid could be used to build a wall three meters high by 0.3 meters thick around the entire country of France. In terms of height, the pyramid was originally 147 meters high, but today the top ten meters are missing, and the entire outer limestone covering has been stripped away. It seems that local builders and conquerors found it convenient to strip off the limestone from the pyramids and use it to build with.

The Great Pyramid of Khufu is considered a wonder of ancient architecture. When you look at it, you immediately wonder how on earth the ancient Egyptians ever managed to build such a structure with only basic mathematics, with no modern machinery (such as cranes, bulldozers, and so forth), and with no iron tools. They had to cut the big limestone blocks with tools made of copper, which is a rather soft metal. But they did manage to do it. The ancient Greek historian, Herodotus (that's H–e–r–o–d–o–t–u–s)—Herodotus said that 400,000 men worked for twenty years to build the Great Pyramid. Archaeologists today doubt these figures, but, of course, the true statistics cannot ever really be determined. It is thought, though, that at least 100,000 worked to build any single pyramid. Most of these were slaves. They worked on the tombs during times when the Nile River overflowed its banks and covered the fields. The Nile's flooding made farming impossible and made transportation of the stone to the pyramid site easier.

The Second and Third Pyramids of Giza were built by Khufu's successors. The tomb of Khafre is the Second Pyramid of Giza. (Khafre is spelled K–h–a–f–r–e.) It was originally 3 meters lower than the Great Pyramid; however, today it is only 0.8 meters lower. Its present height is 136.2 meters.

The Third Pyramid, built for Menkaure, covers only half the area occupied by the Great Pyramid, and it is only 62.5 meters high. Menkaure is spelled M–e–n–k–a–u–r–e.

None of the later pyramids that were built during the next 13 or 14 centuries were nearly as large or as magnificent as the Pyramids of Giza. And even though pyramid building continued right up into the Eleventh and Twelfth Dynasties (that was up through about 1786 B.C.), it was becoming increasingly clear to the pharaohs and the nobles of Egypt that the pyramid method of burial provided really very little or no protection at all for their royal corpses. The pyramids were, of course, impressive and lasting monuments, but they were all too visible. They invited grave robbers to try to break into them. And so eventually, one of the pharaohs, King Thutmose I, decided to sacrifice publicity for safety in the construction of his House of Eternity. I don't need to spell Thutmose for you, do I? Instead of ordering the construction of a pyramid, Thutmose had his tomb dug out of the rock of a valley far from the Nile River and far from Cairo. The spot he chose was some 11 kilometers from the river on its west bank. The area is now known as the Valley of the Kings. Many pharaohs followed Thutmose's example. After him, most of the pharaohs abandoned above-ground pyramid construction in favor of underground hiding places as the burial places for their precious royal bones. And yet, what is so ironic is that even these tombs did not escape the attacks of the grave robbers—persistent devils that they were!

I'll end this discussion by pointing out that, when the ancient Greeks first saw the Great Pyramids of Egypt, the pyramids were already 2,000 years old. The Greeks called them one of the Seven Wonders of the World. Almost nothing remains of the other six Wonders—the Hanging Gardens of Babylon, the Temple of Diana, and so on, but the three mighty Pyramids of Giza, as well as thirty-two other recognizable pyramids, still stand—monuments to a great and ancient civilization and to man's endless search for eternal recognition and eternal life.

Key to Multiple-Choice Questions (Lecture 15)

1. How long did the civilization of ancient Egypt last?   (b)
2. What is meant by the term "dynasty" as used by the lecturer?   (d)
3. What preoccupied the nobles and kings of ancient Egypt according to the lecture?   (c)
4. Why would pharaohs want to have their remains preserved?   (a)
5. During the First Dynasty, what kind of structure was built to house the pharaoh's mummy?   (a)
6. What are the dates of the First and Second Dynasties?   (b)
7. When was the first known "typical" pyramid built?   (c)
8. For whom was the Step Pyramid constructed?   (d)
9. How many blocks of limestone were used to build the Great Pyramid of Cheops?   (a)
10. How many meters high is the Great Pyramid of Giza today?   (a)
11. Why aren't accurate statistics available about how long it took to construct the Great Pyramid of Khufu?   (c)
12. What is the present height in meters of Khafre's Pyramid, the Second Pyramid of Giza?   (d)
13. Which of the three pyramids of Giza is the lowest in height?   (d)
14. According to the presentation, up until what date did above-ground pyramid building continue in ancient Egypt?   (c)

Key to True–False Statements (Lecture 15)

1. F   The civilization lasted for *more* than 3,000 years.
2. T
3. F   They believed that if a dead body were preserved from decay, the soul would *continue* to exist.
4. T
5. ?   Perhaps some slaves did, but some may not have been so willing to die to accompany their masters into the next world. We really can't determine whether they did or did not.
6. ?   Again, we can't assume the grave robbers were poor people; they may even have been wealthy people or associates of the pharaohs.
7. T   So the lecturer indicated.
8. F   The lecturer expressed slight disgust for the idea. Did you note the sarcasm evident in her voice when she said, "Imagine, a grave robbers' union!"?

9. F It looked like a shoe-*box*.

10. F Zoser was a king; Imhotep was the king's architect.

11. F The Pyramid of Cheops *is* the Pyramid of Khufu.

12. ? This can't be inferred from the information presented, since nowhere is mention made of the dietary habits of the ancient royal Egyptians.

13. F They were built during the *Fourth Dynasty*.

14. F The *largest* block weighed 15,000 kilos.

15. T

16. F He stated that *400,000* men worked to build the Great Pyramid.

17. T

18. ? Maybe she was, and maybe she wasn't. We don't know this from what the lecturer said.

19. T

20. T The lecturer does not state this fact per se, but from all that has been stated, you could infer that the pharaohs were powerful (they could command hundreds of thousands of slaves to build their tombs), and that they were obsessed with the idea of preserving their bodies and riches from the grave robbers.